Bernard King lives is Northampton, Eng
student of the runes and ancient myth
quarter of a century.

The *Elements Of* is a series designed to present high quality introductions to a broad range of essential subjects.

The books are commissioned specifically from experts in their fields. They provide readable and often unique views of the various topics covered, and are therefore of interest both to those who have some knowledge of the subject, as well as those who are approaching it for the first time.

Many of these concise yet comprehensive books have practical suggestions and exercises which allow personal experience as well as theoretical understanding, and offer a valuable source of information on many important themes.

In the same series

THE ELEMENTS OF
THE RUNES

Bernard King

ELEMENT

Shaftesbury, Dorset ● Rockport, Massachusetts
Brisbane, Queensland

First published in Great Britain in 1993 by
Element Books Limited
Shaftesbury, Dorset SP7 8BP

Published in the USA in 1993 by
Element Books, Inc.
PO Box 830, Rockport, MA 01966

Published in Australia in 1993 by
Element Books Limited for
Jacaranda Wiley Limited
33 Park Road, Milton, Brisbane 4064

Reprinted 1994
Reprinted April and September 1995

Cover design by Max Fairbrother
Typeset by The Electronic Book Factory Ltd, Fife, Scotland
Printed and bound in Great Britain by
Biddles Limited, Guildford & King's Lynn

British Library Cataloguing in Publication
data available

Library of Congress Cataloging in Publication
data available

ISBN 1–85230–420–0

CONTENTS

This book is dedicated to the memory of
Egil Skallagrimsson
of Borg in Iceland (c.910–990),
possibly the greatest Runemaster
who ever lived.

ACKNOWLEDGEMENTS

I am especially grateful for the inspiration and encouragement offered by Freya Aswynn throughout the preparation of this book. Some few parts of its contents have previously appeared in articles for the publications *Talking Stick* and *Chaos International*.

INTRODUCTION

While there have been books on Vikings, and books on runes, and books on ancient magical practices, there is nothing available outside the shelves of musty and learned libraries which combines the three to give an accurate impression of the life of the people who used the runes, and are still using them, over a period in excess of two thousand years.

This is neither a how-to-do-it book nor yet another collection of ethereal speculations. It conveys at least the flavour of the runes, the script of a people which dominated the north for several hundred years. Its greatest king, Knut (Canute), ruled the three substantial kingdoms of England, Denmark and Norway for the first and only time in history. Its greatest explorers and travellers reached North America centuries ahead of either Columbus or Amerigo Vespucci. Yet both the mythology and the script have been stoically ignored, or treated to rash speculation by outsiders, for far too long.

Any book claiming to offer the elements of a subject supposes more than the usual relationship between author and reader. It assumes that the reader has a desire to learn something more about a subject in which he or she already has a passing interest. And it also assumes that the author has the experience and competence to assist the reader in this essentially personal process.

Whether any increase in the reader's personal knowledge

eventually takes place depends upon the author's lucidity and the reader's faith in the material presented. This in turn relates ultimately to the reader's faith in the author. For this reason I offer a brief autobiographical sketch here at the beginning so that you have some idea of who and what I am before we start.

I was born Bernard John Howard King in the Barratt Maternity Home, Northampton, England, at 9.10 am on 11 June 1946. This makes me a Gemini with Leo rising. Today I am a professional writer. Before that I was student, teacher, carpet salesman, assistant theatre manager, export executive, landscape gardener, advertising copywriter and press officer, to name some of the most significant career moves. If nothing else, this has given me a wide experience of life and work. I've also been married twice. Through the years I've developed a strong interest in magical matters and am today a Priest of Odin, who is my patron deity and giver of the runes.

My interest in the runes goes back well over a quarter of a century, into the days when runes were considered 'German' and thus, in an England still recovering from the effects of the Second World War, virtually taboo. (I met my first German in 1961 and was surprised to discover that, apart from his accent, he was a normal person.) Even as late as 1972 I saw a warehouse worker, who had come over before the war as a refugee from Germany, shudder when he saw a rune used as part of a shipping-mark.

Because of this attitude, information was hard to come by, unlike today with its explosion of interest and literature on the subject. This meant, for me, a great deal of time spent digging in libraries and museums, chasing references in rare and fabled tomes, making notes from authors who frequently contradicted one another, and generally having to learn the hard way.

Yet despite this, the runes soon became the keystone of my life and have haunted and pursued me through the years. Much of the original research I undertook has since been duplicated and published by others, with Freya Aswynn and Edred Thorsson being among the most notable.

In recent years I've had eight fantasy and horror novels published in the UK, three of which have been hardbacked in the States and a further two are to be published in Poland. This book is my first venture into non-fiction, and it has been undertaken because I believe that the information I've accumulated can be of interest and help to many other people.

So much for me. The next question is why anyone today should wish to concern themselves with the runes. This can best be answered by pointing to the enormous upsurge in interest in the subject which has taken place in recent years. Harder to define, and left for later, are the reasons which lie behind this upsurge.

As the twentieth century draws to its close, the runes are reaching a wider audience than at any time in the past thousand years. However, this audience is not the one for which they were originally intended, and this has resulted in many different perspectives emerging and converging upon them.

Runes were originally designed to be used for both secular inscriptions and magical purposes within the culture which valued them. Today they are an object of curiosity and study for the academic, be he or she archaeologist, historian or philologist. They are an object of speculation for the magically inclined, who weave complex and fascinating webs about them, either looking too hard for things that aren't there to find, or merely ripping them off as yet another specious species of psychic fair divinatory technique, without bothering to examine them further. To say that this is true in every case would be inaccurate, but one or the other certainly appears to hold true for the majority.

Astrologers and witches are writing pot-boilers and money-spinners about the runes without really understanding what they are dealing with. Scholars are undecided as to whether the runes had any demonstrable magical content or not, and seem to rest content in scoring points off one another in virtually unreadable papers. The greatest bar to runic studies is that there is no middle ground available for the really interested and enquiring reader. Hitherto the runes have been a subject which either nutty occultists or nutty professors are concerned with, holding no place or interest for a wider, uninformed majority that has so far been condemned to stay that way.

In this century the runic renaissance unfortunately has associations with a prolonged and terrible conflict, and many unwarranted assumptions which should never have arisen have clouded the issue still further. The reference, of course, is to Nazism, and an unjustified association of northern religion with fascism still lingers in many minds. Yet there is nothing racist in northern literature, unless its failure to discriminate positively is taken to imply one. Moreover the Nazi swastika is not an exclusively northern symbol. It may be banned in Germany today, but it's still in current use among the peoples of India. It adorned the spines of every book by Rudyard Kipling until his reaction against its fascist use made him request his publishers to discontinue it. The swastika's adoption by Adolf Hitler (born a Christian, died a Christian) was as a result of a design presented to him in 1920 by a dentist. Runes were studied by branches of the official Nazi party machine and appeared on some Nazi insignia, but all occult or magical movements were banned by the Nazis in the early '30s, when the State became Germany's only acceptable religion.

The net result was to create a popular connection which persists, unjustified, to this day. The revival of Odinism in England has been a rather sad affair because of this association. The Odinist scene seems to be saturated with men professing to worship Odin and Thor, with very little feminine input to balance the perspective. Considering the role of woman in northern society, this is something which needs to be rectified before any revival can proceed with certainty.

The ideal approach is a non-political balance between scholarship and an awareness of the innate magic of the runes. In order to achieve this a great deal of new research has been undertaken, which is being shared in book form for the first time anywhere. If the Northern Mysteries are to take their rightful place in the history of thought, religion and

mysticism, that balance must be recognized and maintained by
every person who chooses to become involved with them.

PLEASE NOTE

There is no single book which can ever tell you everything you
want to know about the runes. Exploring the runes is a highly
personal quest which involves making decisions for yourself,
and because of this you will need both time and intuition in
order to appreciate them.

The runes have a potency of their own which, to anyone
who has ever had any close contact with them, is undeniable.
Their strength can become your strength, but not without
your providing a substantial degree of personal flexibility
and effort.

Making a commitment to the runes and the faith which lies
behind them involves discovering a whole new way of life. The
full potency of these ancient symbols has yet to be discovered,
and only those prepared to be committed to the quest will
come close to a full appreciation of what they have to offer.

1 · THE ORIGIN OF THE RUNES

As historical and archaeological items, the runes show up over a period extending from 200 BC to the late Middle Ages (and into the present) in an area from Iceland to Romania, from the Baltic to the Mediterranean. When we consider that the runes were never used as a pen-and-ink script (except as the toy for scholars they became in later centuries), but only as symbols cut or engraved upon wood, bone, metal and stone, this wide geographical spread is truly remarkable and says a great deal for their appeal and durability.

There's a tendency to dismiss runes as simply the Dark Age script used by those northern peoples who hadn't been converted to Christianity and thus hadn't learned the *monkalpha*, or Latin alphabet. This is unfortunate for many reasons, because simply dismissing the runes as a pagan alphabet denies many of their other functions.

WHERE THE RUNES CAME FROM

At various times over the past 150 years scholars have postulated a variety of origins for the runes. One theory is that they originated from Greek cursive script migrating north.

Another is that they are based on the Latin alphabet, and this at least has the merit of some superficial similarities in the letter forms, especially when we consider that the angular shapes of the runes come from them being cut, not written. Had they been a pen-and-ink script the similarities might have increased dramatically. The theory most often cited is that the runes derive from a North Italic alphabet. Certainly there appears some merit in this when the archaeological evidence is taken into account, for example the inscription on the Negau helmet, one of twenty-six found near the Austro-Yugoslav frontier in 1812, dated variously between 500 BC and AD 1.

Despite the fact that the inscription is in a North Italic script, the words themselves, read from right to left, form a Germanic votive inscription: *Harigast i Teiva*, interpreted as 'from Harigast to Teiva' (probably a version of the Norse warrior-God Tyr).

Yet there are other, less clear-cut ideas which need to be explored. The runes also bear a strong similarity to various symbols of the *hällristningar*, the prehistoric cult symbols used by the northern peoples and found recorded on rock-carvings. And no matter what the origin of the runes, there is the vexed question of who was the first person actually to use the script. Was it designed by committee or created as the work of one inspired individual? We shall most probably never know, and that in itself adds to the power and mystery of the script.

THE GOTHIC CONNECTION

Other authorities have conjectured that the script was derived from the Goths of southern Russia, because three of the earliest extant inscriptions have been found on spearheads discovered

Figure 1. *The Negau helmet inscription*

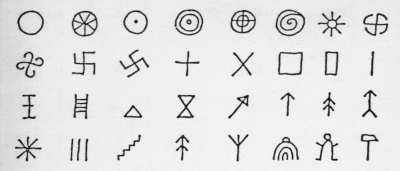

Figure 2. Symbols from the hällristningar

along the route connecting them with their tribal cousins in the Baltic area. The Gothic alphabet was invented by Wulfila (circa AD 311–383), Bishop of Lower Moësia for about forty years, and several scholars seeking his inspiration have in turn derived the letter-forms he created from the runes.

THE RUNIC ALPHABET

FUTHARK OR FUTHORK?

Runic alphabets are usually known as futharks or futhorks. In the way that the alphabet takes its name from the first two letters of the Greek letter-run (α *alpha* and β *beta*), so the runic alphabet takes its name from the sound values of the first six letters, F, U, Th, A, R, K, or in later scripts F, U, Th, O, R, K.

As with any living script, the original developed over the years in different ways. Because of this there are three main variants of the runic alphabet. The original and oldest is known to scholars as the Common Germanic Futhark, and consists of twenty-four symbols with name-words and sound-equivalents. In comparatively late runic times, around AD 800, variants appeared in Anglo-Saxon England and Viking Scandinavia. The Anglo-Saxon runic script increased in number from twenty-four to twenty-eight or even thirty-three symbols. The Viking script, however, reduced to sixteen.

Both these variations are attributed to linguistic changes requiring the original symbols to be revised, but there is evidence to show that the original twenty-four rune script continued to be used for magical purposes.

Rune poems exist which have survived the centuries and have given us meanings and attributions for the letter-forms. They cover the Anglo-Saxon and variants of the Viking scripts only, as the Common Germanic Futhark, which fell out of common use around the year 800, before information began to be recorded in the monkalpha, has no surviving poem.

The three main variants of the runic alphabet are illustrated in Figures 4 and 5 below. In the case of the Viking Futhork, the ambiguous fourth letter is taken as O for this book, as A is represented later in the same rune-run.

There is a fourth variation on the runes, known as the Armanen script. This was basically the work of one Guido von List. Born in 1848, he added the 'von' to give himself a more aristocratic and authoritarian aspect than the son of a Viennese dealer in leather goods might otherwise have expected to command. List was a German occultist who had the system revealed to him during enforced blindness following an eye operation in 1902. The best that can be said of the Armanen system is that it forms the basis of most Nazi rune-lore and is as suspect in its origins as it is in its applications.

THE ÆTTIR

All three of the main runic alphabets described above were divided into three groups of letters called *ættir*, from the Old Icelandic word *ætt*. This is usually taken to have a variety of meanings, including sex, gender, family and eight. 'Eight' is the significant word for our purposes, for quite early on the Common Germanic Futhark was divided into three groups of eight runes each.

Again, evidence for the name is late, as it only appeared as far as modern researchers can ascertain during the seventeenth century. But the division into *ættir* is found on objects as early

Figure 3. The Vadstena bracteate

as the Vadstena and Grumpan bracteates (circa AD 500), and several methods of runic cryptography which grew up in the Viking period (after AD 800) also depend upon the division of the futhark into ættir.

The importance of this division is shown by the fact that both the Viking and Anglo-Saxon runic scripts, neither of which contains twenty-four letters, were subjected to a similar division into three parts. The sixteen rune Viking script was divided into groups of six, five and five.

In Iceland (settled from AD 870 onwards) the runes were gathered into ættir named after Freya, Hagal and Tiw. Tiw, or Tyr, was a favoured deity for giving protection in battle. One of the Sjaelland bracteates names Tyr three times in an inscription to give the wearer good luck. Three was also a potent magical number, together with eight, and the use of the ættir in the Common Germanic Futhark presupposes a magical as well as a secular use for the script. These early uses of the division into ættir show that while the name itself might be late the actual practice was comparatively early.

The symbols illustrated in Figures 4 and 5 are those which are most commonly encountered. To avoid complicating our subject any further, this book uses the original script of twenty-four runes, which will be referred to from now on as the futhark.

The first two columns show the received name of the rune and its most likely translation. The use of a capital and lower case letter together, as with Th, signifies the sound of the single runic letter transliterated into English.

THE WORD 'RUNE'

Different interpretations have been put forward for the meaning of 'rune', yet they all show similarities and impart a rather magical flavour. In early English and related languages it meant a mystery or secret, preserved in the now archaic expression of to 'rown' or 'round' in the ear, or whisper. As with ætt (see above) it has been argued that 'rune' is a comparatively modern term. Yet we know that the people who used the runes themselves applied the term, and there are ancient inscriptions to support this:

Einang Stone (circa 350) — *runo faihido*, painted runes.
Järsberg Stone (circa 450) — *runoz waritu*, engraved runes.
Noleby Stone (circa 450) — *runo fahi*, stain the runes.

In Old German, *runa* also had the meaning of mystery or secret. In Old Norse, it derived from *runar*, a magical sign. Rune may be connected with 'rowan', the folk-name for the mountain ash, referred to in the *Prose Edda* as 'Thor's salvation'. Quickbeam, a possible reference to Thor's thunderbolts, is another name for the same tree.

THE NAMES OF THE RUNES

The lists of rune-names we have are all comparatively late. One source, the *Vienna Codex*, is dated to around 800. The oldest English name list is from the late eighth or early ninth century. The Cotton manuscript containing the text of the Anglo-Saxon rune poem was not written before AD 1000, and the earliest Norse catalogue, the *Abecedarium Nordmannicum*, is ninth century.

THE ELEMENTS OF THE RUNES

COMMON GERMANIC FUTHARK

Name	Meaning	Symbol	
FEHU	cattle	F	ᚠ
URUZ	aurochs	U	ᚢ
THURISAZ	giant	Th	ᚦ
ANSUZ	god	A	ᚨ
RAIDO	riding	R	ᚱ
KAUNAZ	torch	K	ᚲ
GEBO	gift	G	ᚷ
WUNJO	perfection	W	ᚹ
HAGALAZ	hail	H	ᚺ
NAUTHIZ	need	N	ᚾ
ISA	ice	I	ᛁ
JERA	year	J	ᛃ
EIHWAZ	yew	Y	ᛇ
PERTHO	vagina?	P	ᛈ
ALGIZ	protection	Z	ᛉ
SOWULO	sun	S	ᛋ
TEIWAZ	Tyr	T	ᛏ
BERKANA	birch	B	ᛒ
EHWAZ	horse	E	ᛖ
MANNAZ	man	M	ᛗ
LAGUZ	water	L	ᛚ
INGUZ	Ing/Frey	Ng	ᛜ
OTHILA	inheritance	O	ᛟ
DAGAZ	day	D	ᛞ

ANGLO-SAXON FUTHORK

Name	Meaning	Symbol	
FEOH	wealth	F	ᚠ
UR	aurochs	U	ᚢ
ThORN	thorn	Th	ᚦ
OS	god/mouth	O	ᚩ
RAD	riding	R	ᚱ
CEN	torch	C	ᚳ
GYFU	generosity	G	ᚷ
WENNE	bliss	W	ᚹ
HAEGL	hail	H	ᚻ
NYD	trouble	N	ᚾ
IS	ice	I	ᛁ
GER	summer	J	ᛄ
EOH	yew	Y	ᛇ
PEORD	chessman	P	ᛈ
EOLH	sedge	Z	ᛉ
SIGEL	sun	S	ᛋ
TIR	Tyr	T	ᛏ
BEORC	birch	B	ᛒ
EH	horse	E	ᛖ
MAN	man	M	ᛗ
LAGU	ocean	L	ᛚ
ING	Ing	Ng	ᛝ
EThEL	estate	OE	ᛟ
DAEG	day	D	ᛞ
AC	oak	A	ᚪ
AESC	ash	AE	ᚫ
YR	bow?	Y	ᛡ
IAR	otter?	IO	ᛣ
EAR	grave?	EA	ᛠ

Figure 4. Common Germanic and Anglo-Saxon runes

VIKING FUTHORK

Name	Meaning	Symbol	
FE	wealth	F	ᚠ
UR	drizzle	U	ᚢ
ThURS	giant	Th	ᚦ
OSS	god	O	ᚬ
REID	riding	R	ᚱ
KAUN	ulcer	K	ᚴ
HAGALL	hail	H	ᚼ
NAUD	constraint	N	ᚾ
ISS	ice	I	ᛁ
AR	plenty	A	ᛅ
SOl	sun	S	ᛋ
TYR	Tyr	T	ᛏ
BJARKAN	birch	B	ᛒ
MADR	man	M	ᛘ
LOGR	water	L	ᛚ
YR	bow?	Z	ᛦ

Figure 5. Viking runes

Both the Icelandic and Norwegian rune poems are substantially later in date, the latter from the late twelfth and the former from the fifteenth century. Yet it is from these sources that the names of the runes are derived. As the earliest of these was set down some 700 years after the beginnings of runic usage, the origins of the names cannot really be regarded as anything more than scholarly speculation. In fairness it needs to be pointed out that all of the runic poems must derive from earlier oral originals, and that the runes themselves were the only form of writing available at the time of the poems' inception.

The runes would have originally received their names at a time when the Germanic world (which includes Scandinavia) was both relatively united and unanimously pagan. Two factors would have determined any single name. Firstly, the name of the rune would serve as a mnemonic or memory-aid to call both the symbol and the sound to mind. Secondly, the name would also serve to recall and record significant details of tribal life.

WHO USED THE RUNES?

Today we think of literacy as a common skill, with those who can't read or write being very much in the minority, whatever we may think of the schools system. But at the time when the runes were current in the north, literacy of any kind was very much the exception. Most people, faced with a futhark inscription, wouldn't have known where to begin, even if they recognized most of the shapes of the letters. Yet the script was very much in demand, even from people who didn't know one end of a rune from another, and archaeological finds exist with shapes that mimic runes cut into them, demonstrating that even then demand could outstrip supply.

We tend to think of runes either as something Viking, a warrior script cut and read by berserkers and conquerors, or as a mystical, magical alphabet which was the exclusive preserve of sorcerers and witches. Both ideas are right, but they are also wrong.

Runes were learned and used by individuals, who might have been scholars, poets, farmers, sorcerers, warriors, witches or even lawyers and diplomats, not to mention merchants. They learned their runes from someone who already knew them, whatever that person's occupation or gender might have been. Magic in the north was mostly taught by women, be they foster-mothers, wives, witches or queens. Only one instance in the sagas, the Dark Age tales of Scandinavia, shows a woman being taught by men, and that woman, Gunnhild Orm's-daughter, went on to become three times a queen, three times an exile and the greatest witch the northlands ever knew. She was taught by Lapps, and the Lappish and Finnish peoples were famous for their magical knowledge in Viking times.

Because the knowledge required to use the futhark, either for magical or secular purposes, was essentially specialist, the runecutter or runemaster was a valued member of society. Runecutters and runemasters were different people, the former being competent to read and cut them, and the latter knowing the full magical power of the futhark in addition to having the former's skills. Don't think that because I've used the term 'runemaster' women were excluded. As far back as Tacitus, the Germanic peoples were known to have believed that a special gift of wisdom and prophecy resided in woman, and woman's role in northern society was respected in a way that feminists today would have applauded. The bride-price came from man to woman, divorce was freely available, women owned their own property and were full members of society in every respect. They were as free to learn the runes as men, and frequently did.

WHAT WERE RUNES USED FOR?

Historical evidence shows that runes were used in a variety of ways on a variety of materials. Let's look at a few examples.

A clasp dated to around 600 found at Charnay, France, bears an inscription meaning 'To my husband, Iddo. Liano'. It was most probably a present, and while Liano may have known and cut the runes herself it was most probably engraved for her, in the same way that we'd have a jeweller engrave a watch or locket today.

A bracteate, or coin-like medallion, from a century earlier and further north in Poznan, Poland, is inscribed 'wise one, runes' and could be regarded as a magical teaching aid to help the wearer learn his or her runes better.

From Oppland in Norway comes a spearhead dated around 175 inscribed 'prober'. The inscription here was most probably cut to reinforce the weapon magically, giving both it and its owner an 'edge' in battle.

Twenty runes of a futhark were cut around 550 on a marble column found in Breza, Yugoslavia. This could have been a practice-piece, possibly even a teaching aid, with the runemaster or carver cutting the runes as a demonstration. The full futhark is known to have been used for magical purposes, but that's unlikely to have been the case here.

A standing stone from Bohuslän, Sweden, is dated to around 600 and is inscribed 'Hariwulf's monument'. This is a memorial, though not necessarily a grave-marker. Memorials are often found to people who have been buried elsewhere.

From these early examples we begin to get some idea of the uses to which runic inscriptions were put. In later times more wooden examples are found undecayed, and the secular uses widen even further to include almanacs, merchants' tallies and even love-letters.

THE RUNEMASTERS

Despite the comparative wealth of inscriptions which have survived, we know very little about any of the individuals who inscribed runes on such a wide variety of objects over a recorded period in excess of 1500 years. While we frequently know their names, for it wasn't uncommon for runestones and objects to be signed, our knowledge mostly stops there. Only occasionally, as with the witch Thurid in *Grettir's Saga*, or Egil Skallagrimsson, the poet-farmer-warrior hero of *Egil's Saga*, do we have any fragment of biography. For the most part, the runemasters remain either anonymous or simply names.

The same is also true for whatever training they underwent. As there was only oral instruction available for most of the period when runes were current, the runemaster was probably apprenticed to one who already had the requisite knowledge and skills. There may have been a craft initiation, perhaps modelled on Odin's self-sacrifice in the poem *Hávamál*, but no details have come down to us so far.

Certainly the training would have involved more than simply learning the shapes and phonetic values of the letters. *Hávamál* provides a synopsis of what the training might have embraced, but doesn't go into details. The runemaster, like Odin himself, would have more than a passing acquaintance with the intricacies of Norse poetry. Ideally he would also know the divinatory uses of the runes and understand the cultic meanings of the symbols. In turn this may have necessitated a knowledge of leechcraft, the numerology behind some of the apparently-nonsensical sequences which show up in many of the extant inscriptions, and the ability to act as something of a philosopher as well.

Ability would have varied widely between individuals, depending as it did upon aptitude and the degree of knowledge possessed by the teacher. So would the ability to recognize and analyse sounds and interpret them as spelling. Virtually all the letter-forms have variants, showing the range of differences between runemasters in received learning as modified by personal belief and preference.

Many inscriptions which have been found are not the work of true runemasters at all, but simply that of ordinary people – craftsmen, merchants and warriors – who acquired the basic skill of cutting runes. Not all the inscriptions are magical, though the common perception of the runemaster's skills would have lent an air of magic to his activities and his persona. This may explain why it is the runemaster's name which appears upon some of the memorial stones, where the name of the person being commemorated doesn't even appear in the inscription.

The inscription of runes was regarded as a traditional craft. The inscription of classical alphabets in their entirety, in much the same way as the futhark is found on the Kylver stone, parallels the use of runes even in Christian times. Yet only the full alphabet, as opposed to single letters or letter sequences, is used for such prophylactic purposes. Runes go beyond this, developing standard formulae and even abbreviated forms in addition to the idiographic use of single runes. This demonstrates that it wasn't sufficient for the runemaster just to know his futhark. He was also required to be sufficiently literate to master the techniques required for full, grammatical inscriptions.

SUPPLY AND DEMAND

The demand for runemasters and runic inscriptions often exceeded the supply available. A cremation urn from the Anglo-Saxon cemetery excavated at Loveden Hill in Lincoln-shire bears rune-like symbols which are definitely not genuine runes. One possible explanation is that no runemaster was available at the time the inscription was required, so someone with a little familiarity was called upon to produce something similar. If this forgery was indeed the explanation, then it shows a knowledge of, and desire for, runic inscriptions by people with no runic literacy, who had to settle for second-best. The Loveden Hill urn is not an isolated example. Similar rune-like inscriptions appear during a long period of history throughout a wide spread of geographical locations.

THE MYTHICAL ORIGIN OF THE RUNES

The Norse poem *Hávamál*, which translates as 'The Words of the High One', contains some sections of great interest to anyone approaching the Northern Mysteries or runecraft. While it is unlikely it was written by Odin himself, as internal evidence points to it being composed around 950, it unashamedly purports to contain his words.

One section requiring examination is that known as the *Runatál*, which deals with Odin's self-sacrifice on the world-ash Yggdrasil in order to obtain the runes. For nine nights, with none giving him food or drink, he hung upon the tree. In addition he bore a self-inflicted spear wound, as a mystical offering of himself to himself. At the culmination of this initiation he looked down and cried out, though whether in pain or triumph is not recorded. Then he snatched up the runes before falling free of his torment.

Myth and history rarely agree, and the origin of the runes preferred by historians has little in common with the *Runatál* version. But the fact remains that the runes were a potent influence upon northern culture and magic, embodying as they do more than just letters of an alphabet. They were in use for more than 1100 years before a series of Christian proscriptions placed upon these overt relics of paganism forced them underground in their homelands. Their exact origin may never be known, but as far as believers in their obvious power are concerned, the *Runatál* embodies the best version yet.

2 · RUNES, RELIGION AND SOCIETY

It's one of the sad facts of our educational and cultural background today, formed as it has been by generations persisting in the belief that the north had little other than barbarity to offer, that the word mythology, for the vast majority, conjures up pictures of Greek or Roman heroes and deities. The labours of Hercules, the travels of Jason or Ulysses, Jove and Zeus taking on animal form for a quick tryst with a fancied maiden – all these are favourites, cleaned up where necessary, for a modern audience that possesses no overt links with them whatsoever. Yet Odin has stalked our historical byways and ridden with the Wild Hunt through the skies above . . . Peterborough? Yes, indeed he did, and there's even a monkish chronicle recording it. The Norse deities were at home in a geographical area covering more than half of England for many years, and are increasingly finding that a welcome is being prepared for them once again. Sites such as Wayland's Smithy in Oxfordshire, named for the old northern hero/god/smith Volund, are no longer mere curiosities. They are beginning to be used as focal points by people increasingly in touch with the old ways and deities.

THE MYTHOLOGY OF THE NORTH

The mythology of the north is rich and colourful. Its characters are as clearly defined, frequently more so, than any to be found in so-called Classical myth. It also has a greater relevance for anyone wanting to take their beliefs and traditions from the land they inhabit, or the ethnic background to which they belong. It has stories to tell which are the equal of anything in mythology anywhere, such as Thor dressing up as a goddess to get his stolen hammer back, or the binding of the Fenris Wolf, or the fearsome imagery of that last terrible battle at the Ragnarök. These are tales of deities and heroes with more bite and flavour than the legends of the saints of the Christian church, and they are an important part of the long-denied birthright of the northern peoples. Their rediscovery becomes a matter of great personal satisfaction and a source of genuine pleasure.

The pantheon of Norse mythology is actually two that have combined into one, formed of the Æsir and the Vanir. The Æsir on the whole tend to be related to Odin, such as Thor, Baldur and Frigg. The Vanir centre on Njord and his two best-known children, Frey and Freya, whose names mean 'lord' and 'lady.' Basic information on some of the gods and goddesses is given below.

Baldur is the beautiful God, son of Odin and Frigg. He is killed by a shaft of mistletoe, all other created things having sworn not to harm him, and descends into Hel (which is spelled with one L) with his wife Nanna beside him. After the Ragnarök he rises again. His function in the pantheon is actually minimal, despite the power which later generations have ascribed to him by comparisons with Christ.

Frey, son of Njord, is very much the patron of fertility, ruler of the realm of the light elves responsible for the growth of vegetation. He is the noblest of the brave gods and the patron of summer sunshine. His main attribute is his erect penis, but despite this he's probably the closest northern equivalent to the more politely-fertile horned God of Wicca.

Freya Frey's sister, is the most renowned of the goddesses and the patroness of war, love and witchcraft. Although Frigg is Odin's wife (one of at least three), Freya is both Odin's opposite polarity and most complementary partner. She and Odin share the dead slain in battle, with Freya getting first pick. The most beautiful of the deities, she's never above a little pragmatic whoring, as when she sleeps with four dwarves in one night to pay for the necklace Brisingamen which they had made for her.

Frigg is Odin's wife and the mother figure of Norse mythology. Renowned for her knowledge, she's also famed for never giving anything away, not even to her husband. She even knows the eventual fate of her son Baldur, heroically and vainly trying to forestall it. Frigg was usually depicted as a tall, stately woman, beautiful in her white dress and heron-plumes. As the patroness of the northern housewife and mother she carried a set of keys at her girdle. Frigg and Freya tend to blur together in some aspects of the myths, as they embrace complementary aspects of the archetypal woman, certainly in so far as most male mythographers are concerned.

Heimdal is the shining God, guardian of the rainbow bridge which leads up to Asgard and, as a watchman, possessor of the *Gjallarhorn* which he blows at the onset of the Ragnarök. His hearing is so acute that he can hear the grass grow and even hear wool growing on a sheep's back.

Idun is married to Bragi, the God of Poetry. She has the responsibility for the health of the gods, who are required to eat an apple a day from her ash-wood casket to keep their youth and strength.

Loki would take several books to explore fully. Odin's blood brother, if not actually more closely related, Loki is the trickster of the pantheon, good guy and bad guy in one. Both a help and a menace, he shows up in many of the myths as the God who not only gets people into trouble but, albeit reluctantly, also gets them out of it. A fiery figure, he very probably has some giant in his ancestry, as does Odin himself.

Njord is the God of the sea and the patron of sailors and fishermen. The father-figure of the Vanir, he is the bestower of riches as well as a brave and seasoned warrior. He married the Goddess Skadi, who chose him in a contest, mistaking him for Baldur because he had such beautiful feet.

Odin is the Allfather, patron of poets, warriors and statesmen and God of the dead, war and magic.. His pragmatism is legendary, and has given rise to false accusations of treachery. He carries the spear Gungnir, which never misses its mark and has runes on the shaft which uphold the law. He rides the eight-legged stallion Sleipnir and gathers warriors to fight beside him at the Ragnarök and feast in Valhalla (literally *Valhöll*, the 'hall of the chosen', where the warriors are served with mead and boar-meat by shield-maidens) until it comes. He won the runes for mankind by an act of personal sacrifice and gave his right eye for wisdom.

Thor is Odin's best-known son. A red-bearded giant-whacker wielding the magic hammer Mjölnir, killing giants seems more a hobby than an occupation for him. Not very bright, but with thunder and lightning in his armoury, he yet succeeds in being soft-hearted and popular and resourceful when he has to be. Odin must have been extremely fond of Thor, the amount of time he spent ragging his son. Thor is married to Sif, the corn-Goddess, and when Loki cuts off Sif's wonderful hair, a wig of spun gold has to be provided until it grows back.

Tyr is the fighting God, the general of the pantheon, whereas Thor is more the foot-soldier and Odin the statesman. Despite his nobility and reputation for straight-dealing, Tyr is forced to swear a false oath when the Fenris Wolf is bound and loses his right hand to the beast as a penalty.

This is a brief and not always reverent look at some of the most prominent members of the Norse pantheon. Anyone who's read this far will either have decided to explore this rich and potent mythology for themselves or throw this book away.

THE NORTHERN PEOPLES

English history, as everyone must know after years of being told it's so, began with the Romans, continued with William the Conqueror, went on with the Wars of the Roses and only really amounted to anything after Henry VIII. And if you believe that you'll believe anything.

In fact, that brief summation of early English history couldn't be further from the truth. There were peoples settled here long before the Romans, and with the collapse of the Roman Empire around 440, and the consequent withdrawal of their occupying forces, the country was open to successive waves of invaders. Most of these could accurately be described as Germanic or Teutonic, and they had a great deal in common with one another. These invaders included Angles, Saxons, Jutes, Danes and Norwegians, sharing a common culture and, wherever Christianity didn't intrude, similar religious and social values. England's best-known Danish king, Knut (Canute), actively campaigned for Norway's first native-born saint and martyr, King Olaf, to be created, whilst experiencing a variety of difficulties with the English Church. Knut was far too busy holding together an empire consisting of England, Denmark and Norway to sit around seashores ordering anything as recalcitrant as water about, and the fact that this fable is the best-known legacy of his reign is proof of the denigration of the period to which historians previously subjected it.

William the Conqueror himself was only about a hundred years away from his Norwegian roots. When Norway was being unified under the rule of King Harald Fairhair in the 930s many chieftains took exception to his policies. Unfortunately for them, Harald was dealing from a position of great strength, leaving them with a choice between suicidal opposition or voluntary exile. This is one of the main reasons for the colonization of Iceland, discovered by the Scandinavians around 870, though previously known to both the Irish and the Romans, and helps to explain why so many Norse traditions have been preserved as a part of Icelandic culture. Indeed, modern Icelandic is virtually identical to the Old Norse language, which has aided immeasurably with the translation and interpretation of runic inscriptions and surviving Old Norse texts.

One of the chieftains exiling himself and his followers from Norway to escape Harald Fairhair's rule was known as Hrolf the Ganger. He and his people took ship and carved out a piece of northern France for their new domain. It was subsequently named Normandy, which is etymologically not a million miles from 'Realm of the North Men', and its most famous inhabitant invaded England in 1066.

Such is a brief overview of the English connection. Let's not forget that the Danelaw covered half the country, and that the Viking kingdom of Northumbria, with its capital at Jorvik (York), was only finally obliterated by a coalition of English and Scots forces, unusually for the times working together, during the 950s. There were also Viking presences in Ireland, the Orkneys, the Shetlands, the Faeroes, the Isle of Man, Lancashire and many other parts of these islands, all making their input to the existing culture over a 600 year period between the Roman withdrawal and the Norman invasion. Neither did Viking activity cease after William, with the last recorded raid on these shores taking place in the 1170s.

The Viking activity on and around our own shores was paralleled in many other parts of the northern hemisphere. Iceland was colonized, as was Greenland. Expeditions reached North America 500 years ahead of Columbus. As well as Norway, Sweden and Denmark, today regarded as the Viking homelands, parts of Russia and other Baltic states were inhabited by the same culture. This is also true for Germany and Holland. And on the eastern front, the Emperor of Byzantium's famed bodyguard, the Varangian Guard, consisted entirely of Viking mercenaries.

All this serves to demonstrate how widespread the culture of the northern peoples was. At the same time as being the fierce warriors of legend and fact ('From the fury of the Northmen, O Lord, deliver us . . .' said the English Missal) they displayed many traits which still have great relevance. Religious toleration was one which both Christian and Islamic 'fundies' might usefully adopt today. Despite the breadth of their travels, there is no recorded or even legendary instance of their attempting to convert any of the peoples they had contact with to their own religion. Even among themselves there was great diversity, both within and without the Norse pantheon. Frey and Thor were probably the most popular deities, each with his own cult and mysteries, and no overt rivalry between worshippers. Odin, usually regarded as a warrior God, also held the title Allfather, heading the pantheon with a greater sympathy and benevolence than most of the fictional and Hollywood representations ascribe to him. Should anyone choose to worship no deity, or even profess atheist views, this was entirely up to him or her, with no pressure or social stigma attaching to the decision.

LIFE AND AFTERLIFE

The here and now was just as important to the Norseman as the afterlife, contrasting with the attitude of many Christians who ruled their lives here according to the received idea of the hereafter. The Norseman, or woman, was aware of the future life and held its prospect dear, certainly more dear than that of dishonour in mortal form. Yet, at the risk of seeming repetitive, they were a pragmatic people, both ready and willing to make the best of any situation, natural or supernatural.

If you did well in the here then there was a place for you in Valhalla in the future, eating pork and drinking to your heart's content. The position of woman in this warrior's heaven is never made clear in the surviving texts, but there is no reason to think that the Germanic women, so close to their men even in battle, were denied an equal share of the afterlife. If your works were insignificant or unworthy, then you would end up in Hel. But even this was not a punishment as such, and even the God Baldur ended in Hel before the Ragnarök, or Doom of the Gods. It simply meant you would have to try harder to find a place in Valhalla, putting the effort into the afterlife that you hadn't made whilst in a fleshly incarnation.

THE EFFECT OF CHRISTIANITY

The coming of Christianity to the north was a slow process. England was Christianized early, and the pragmatism of the invaders following upon the Roman withdrawal, coupled with their natural tolerance, permitted its continuance and growth. Viking traders were able to deal with Christians, provided they accepted *primsigning*, which is best described as a promise to think about becoming Christian eventually. This was a practice widely adopted for trade with the English, who, despite their longer acquaintance with the new faith, retained sufficient of their original Norse pragmatism to regard flexibility as a virtue when there was benefit to be derived from it, and were not slow to employ anything that might serve to mutual advantage. And as with England today, where there is a state religion and a variety of private faiths, Norse paganism was still very much alive on the quiet, even centuries after the Norman conquest.

In Scandinavia, however, things took much longer, with the hand of the *hvitakrist*, the White Christ, only really taking hold after the Battle of Stiklestad in 1030, when the death of King Olaf and his subsequent canonization gave the northern lands their first native-born saint. The coming of Christianity itself was strongly fundamentalist in flavour, with characters such as King Olaf Trygveson of Norway literally demanding the conversion of his contemporaries at sword-point. In 995 Olaf converted the Orkneys by inviting Earl Sigurd and his young son Hindius to meet him aboard his ship, anchored off South Ronaldsay. Once on board Sigurd only agreed to accept the new faith after Olaf had threatened to butcher his son. Later Olaf's favourite conversion technique, threatening the lives of hostages, played a strong role in the conversion of Iceland on 4 June 1000. Even here northern pragmatism played its part, with the old religion being permitted to continue in private and many of the chieftains present at the conversion putting off cold-water baptism then and there in favour of resorting to hot springs on the way home. Yet the old gods surrendered to sleep rather than extermination, as their reawakening today has testified. Iceland officially adopted Norse paganism as a second state religion in the early 1970s, and other northern countries are beginning to follow suit.

Christianity brought both a blessing and a curse to the north, as far as anyone attempting to reconstruct the times is concerned. Before its arrival, written literacy was reserved for those competent to read and write runes. With its coming, however, the *monkalpha* or Latin alphabet arrived, and written accounts were constructed for the first time since Tacitus wrote the *Germania* in the latter years of the first century AD. These have ensured the survival of a great deal of information and literature, but the material was preserved in many cases two or three hundred years after its original composition and with a Christian taint permeating its northern flavour. This requires identifying, if not eradicating, before much of the practical information given about religious and magical practices can be accurately reconstructed, rather than attempting to use it straight with its bias intact. One prime example is the humanization of the gods and goddesses in the opening chapters of Snorri Sturluson's *Ynglinga Saga*, where the myths are turned into pseudo-history for the edification of Christian readers and Odin, Frigg and others appear as mortals.

WOMEN IN NORTHERN SOCIETY

In dealing with historical data it may appear that a modern myth is being perpetuated, in that there has been no mention so far of the role of women in northern society. But to assume that they were either insignificant or unimportant would be a dreadful mistake. Behind every great man there was indeed a great woman, be she mother, lover, sister, wife or even foster-mother. Women in the northlands weren't just the little home-makers that myth has turned them into. In the same way that goddesses such as Freya, Frigg, Idun, Sif and many others play important parts in the mythology and religion of the north, so northern women constituted a vital aspect of northern society and history.

From the time of Tacitus through to that of Snorri Sturluson, a period of some 1100 years and more, woman had an influential role which was both welcomed and respected by the menfolk. The reason it isn't better-known today is basically that recorded history dealing with the times came from the pens of monkish historians, and Christianity has ever had a love-hate affair with women, either turning them into unemotional plaster saints or ultimately damned objects of derision. Certainly the one thing they were never allowed to be by these commentators was influential. But despite this bias and its clouding effect through the centuries, there is sufficient surviving evidence to show that women in the north had the devotion of their men, and consideration bordering upon the idealised chivalry of the Middle Ages.

If we strip away the historical and sexist overtones to which woman has been subjected, we rediscover a culture where woman was completely equal to man, owning property in her own right and being treated with love and respect. The dowry, usually thought of today as being brought from wife to husband, was brought from husband to wife. And the Goddess Freya was the prime exponent and teacher of *seidr*, one of the most important and least-understood branches of northern magic, with her best-known student being Odin himself. The total equality of woman covered every social and religious level, and as far back as Tacitus we find women regarded as possessing an element of holiness and a gift for prophecy. Man neither scorned to ask woman's advice, nor lightly disregarded her replies.

Unfortunately even modern exponents of the Northern Mysteries can be found propagating the inferior role of women, thus denigrating their frequently substantial achievements in other areas. But in order to create a balanced reconstruction of Norse practices we have to re-enter their society in so far as we are able. The culture of the time was based upon a strong sense of freedom, but with personal liberty being balanced by a thorough appreciation of the need for responsibility and self-regulation. Equality was based upon merit, with even slaves having their rights as well as their obligations and being permitted to own their own property. The only obligation was to offer a share of the harvest to the master, making them more like tenants than the down-trodden and frequently crushed pyramid-builders of Egypt.

THE IMAGE OF THE NORSEMAN

The Viking image, so beloved of fantasy writers, is based on three important factors. One is the land inhabited by the people, a land of harsh winters, rocky fjords and icy waters, which sent them abroad in search of territorial acquisitions. Another is the previously-mentioned Christian bias, with the pragmatic nature of the northern peoples being woefully and sometimes deliberately misunderstood. Most Viking raids began as trading voyages, but if they encountered weaklings they could rip off they were hardly averse to doing so. After all, these wretches were outside the society and culture the Norse peoples belonged to.

The Vikings especially had, and still have, a reputation for rape and pillage. Rapes very probably took place as an early version of a sailor having a wife in every port, and we should not forget that these people were among the greatest seafarers of the Dark Ages. Homosexual rape was occasionally used to shame enemies. Pillage was simply the result of a realization that the people they had set out to trade with were weak and could be stolen from with impunity. Again, simple pragmatism would dictate their actions. As with every other people of the ancient world, including the highly civilized Egyptians, who sacrificed redheads out of hand, whatever you did to those outside your own society was both acceptable and proper. There would be no karmic debt accruing or vengeful Yahweh to placate. You behaved as was accepted by your peers and felt no guilt, exactly as the British Raj did on occasions in India.

This leads us to the third factor, the culture itself. This was based on strength, and interfering outsiders were dealt with harshly and often efficiently, as even the Romans discovered. And yet, as anyone who has examined that culture already knows, it was also rich in art and poetry, with fine literature and beautiful objects surviving into our own times, many of both intimately connected with the runes. The runic script was much more than just an alphabet. To term it a northern Qabala is both praise and disservice, for the differences outweigh the similarities and the cultures creating each differ too widely. The runes are at the heart of the Northern Mysteries.

3 · THE SCOPE OF NORTHERN MAGICAL PRACTICE

That the runes were an integral part of Norse religion is indisputable. They are mentioned in most of the significant surviving poems of the period, as well as in most of the sagas written down later from oral sources. Regarded as the gift of Odin, chief deity of the pantheon, they were both a holy and secular script at the same time.

It's hard for us to conceive of a time when writing was the prerogative of the few rather than the gift of education to the many. But that is exactly the situation which obtained in the Viking Age and earlier with regard to the runes. The art of writing was reserved for the few, and we may imagine the apparently magical effect it would have, with scratched marks turning into words which could be repeated again and again without changing.

This mix of the holy and the secular was emphasized by the knowledge which permitted its utilization being held in the hands of a comparative few. The runemaster could take your words and immortalize them. He or she, and we must never forget that there is evidence for women knowing their runes as well as men, engraved whatever you wanted in such a way that it could be repeated by those few who knew the script. Such a skill would have appeared almost supernatural to the many who were ignorant of its practice, and the esteem in which the runemaster was held is the easier to understand if we take account of this.

THE RUNATÁL

ODIN AND THE RUNES

The Norse poem called *Runatál* clearly divides into at least two distinct sections, both of which are highly relevant for any understanding of northern magic and runecraft. The first verses deal with the introductory matter, which involves Odin's winning of the runes by hanging for nine days and nights on the world-tree Yggdrasil:

> I know I hung on the wind-swept tree,
> Its roots to the wise unknown;
> Spear-pierced, for nine long nights,
> To Odin pledged, self offered to self,
>
> They gave no bread, nor drinking horn;
> Down into the depths I gazed:
> Crying aloud I took up runes,
> Then finally I fell.
>
> Nine powerful songs from Bolthorn's son,
> Bestla's famous father,
> I learned; he poured me precious mead
> Of magic Odraerir.
>
> Learned I grew in hidden lore.
> Prospering in wisdom;
> Word from word bestowed a word,
> And deed from deed new doings.
>
> You will find runes, and right read staves,
> Strong staves, mighty staves of sages,
> Staves that Bolthorn stained,
> Graven great by Odin.

For Æsir by Odin, for elves by Dain,
By Dvalin for the dwarves,
By Asvid too for hated giants,
And some made for myself:

Thund, before man was made, scratched them,
Who rose first, fell thereafter.

The eighth verse in particular is notable:

Know how to cut, know how to read,
Know how to stain, know how to prove,
Know how to ask and sacrifice,
And how to send and to destroy.

The ninth verse rounds things off with some advice which is
sound by any religion's standards:

Ask not rather than over-pledge,
Gift ever looks for gift;
Best sent not than wasted: this, ere man,
Wrote Thund, risen, returning.

INSTRUCTIONS FOR WORKING WITH THE RUNES

Eight is one of the principal magical numbers of runic magic,
and the *Runatál* contains a list of eight separate techniques
which must be mastered by the rune magician. Let's examine
these in turn.

The first three techniques to be mentioned, cutting, reading
and staining, are techniques which the ordinary rune carver
would have known, such as the person who cut Hariwulf's
monument on the stone at Bohuslan in Sweden. In fact that
person could have got away with just the first two, which are
inter-connected. In order to cut runes you have to be able to
read them, otherwise what you cut is gibberish. And that's
exactly what is found on some objects, with rune-like shapes
with no meaning replacing the real thing. This demonstrates
either that the demand for runic inscriptions outstripped the
capacities of those who created them, or that the runemaster

was a being of some status, well worth emulating by ambitious characters who didn't have the knowledge.

Cutting

Cutting for magical purposes involved a concentration on the characters being cut to liberate their powers. It would have been a ritual in itself, with the runes being chanted to accompany the action.

Reading

Reading involved knowing the runes and their correspondences, to ensure that what was being cut, be it for secular or magical purposes, was appropriate. There's no evidence to show that the runemaster had to master a Norse equivalent of the Druidic 150 oghams, but certainly there were lists of correspondences which proved essential. There is also a close correspondence to the modern sense of 'reading', namely consulting for divination.

Staining

Staining was dependent upon the material and the purpose. Runic jewellery often had the cut symbols picked out with niello. Standing stones were often painted to bring out the cuts. But for magical purposes the most likely staining medium in the majority of cases was the blood of the runemaster him- or herself, derived by cutting or, in certain female uses, during the monthly courses. There is reason to suppose that semen was also employed on some occasions.

It might be argued that red colouring would suffice in place of blood, but the runes are attributed to Odin, whose sacred colour traditionally is blue. Were colouring sufficient, magical runes would have been stained blue, and the use of a different colour suggests that it is the ingredients rather than the hue which is important. This leads inexorably to the conclusion that blood was used because it was blood, and not because it was a pigment. Red was Thor's favourite colour, and in later times runes are often found dedicated to him for that very reason. In most cases this is inappropriate as Thor's red was emblematic of love, in the same way that the base colour of valentine cards today is always red. Northern brides wore a ring set with a red stone.

The blood used to stain the runes should always be that of the runemaster and no other. If you dare not cut yourself to stain the runes then how will you ever dare to take responsibility for having invoked the powers they represent? The blood links the object to the originator, making it a true extension of his or her desire.

Proving

Proving referred to both the runes being cut and the person doing the cutting. The concept of magical initiation was as valid for a runemaster as for anyone else, and the knowledge imparted orally and in practical demonstration would only have been communicated to the worthy, who would have to 'prove' their worth. And any single inscription, once cut, would need to be proven before it was known to be of use to the runemaster, enabling it to be added to the corpus of knowledge that individual accumulated.

Asking

Again, asking is in a magical context, and relates back to reading. It involved being sufficiently aware of the meanings and correspondences, and the numerology employed in sequence inscriptions as opposed to word inscriptions, to be certain that the charm would perform as intended. Here a similarity to prayer should be noted, though in an invocatory rather than an imploring sense.

Sacrificing

Sacrificing has to do with the consecration of the symbols used, each of which, as well as being a component, made up a magical whole. Again the inference leads us back to the correspondences, this time specifically to the magical power of the symbol within its context.

Sending

Sending refers to the actual activation of the completed rune-charm, the making-it-do-its-job part of the process. Like any other form of spell, a rune-charm needs to be directed, and while this could be assumed in the purposeful way in which the charm is created, the extra reinforcement of the completed charm ensures an inescapable certainty equivalent to a statement of intent.

Destroying

Here, destroying doesn't refer to death magic or cursing, as the object of the charm will already have been established by the symbols employed. Its real meaning relates to the deactivation of an unwanted charm, either by the originator or by another. There is an example in *Egil's Saga* of a badly-cut love charm causing sickness, and the charm having to be destroyed before the victim can begin to recover.

THE RUNATÁL CHARMS

The eighteen *Runatál* charms form the longest extant list of magical practices. Because of its range, this list is the best to work with at this stage. If we examine each charm in turn we will discover its purpose and, in many cases, some hints as to its application.

> 1. A charm I know no king can say
> Nor any man has mastered;
> Help is it called because it aids
> At times of sickness and sorrow.

This charm is a lifter-up of spirits, bringing cheer back during periods of illness or depression. The statement that no-one has mastered it would also apply to the other seventeen, as Odin is speaking, revealing the charms for the first time.

2. Another is there that I know
Which is required for all
The sons of men that would obtain
Knowledge of healing skills.

This is a charm for leechcraft, and complements the first. Its use will enable the user to become skilled in the healing arts.

3. I know a third: in battle's need
It fetters any foe;
It blunts the edge of enemy swords;
Nor wiles nor weapons wound.

Here we have a battle charm, preventing adversaries from harming the possessor in conflict. It would most likely have been worn as a talisman, possibly in such a way, and of such material, to make its presence obvious, thus providing a psychological advantage to the wearer.

4. A fourth I know: if I should find
My limbs bound with strong chains,
I chant the spell that sets me free,
Breaks bonds from feet and hands.

This is a charm which, because it relates to freeing oneself from bonds, does not actually require cutting. The runes could be employed in other ways, as sound vibrations and mental tuning devices, in addition to being cut, stained, etc.

5. I know a fifth: if someone flings
A spear to harm my friends,
It's not so fast but I can stop it
If I see it fly.

A defence charm, this turns a flying missile from its harmful course and sends it harmlessly to earth, assuming it's spotted in time. This charm could be described by a cynic as giving the wearer the ability to dodge.

6. I know a sixth: if one should curse
By cutting runes on roots,

> That one who wished I come to harm
> Will meet his doom, not I.

This is a counter-magic spell. The outlaw Grettir, holed up on Drang Isle off the coast of Iceland, was only killed when his adversary had an old witch cut runes on an uprooted trunk which floated across to the island. Grettir tried to cut the trunk for firewood and the axe was deflected into his leg. The wound festered and he died. Using this charm would have invoked the much-vaunted Law of Return, by which a thwarted spell rebounds upon its caster, and saved Grettir's life at Thurid's expense.

> 7. I know a seventh: if the hall
> Flames high around my friends,
> Though hot the fire and widely spread
> My spell will check its course.

Here we have a fire-extinguisher. Being surrounded and burned in one's hall was unsporting, but common practice if the sagas can be believed, as anyone who's read *Njal's Saga* will know.

> 8. I know an eighth: which everyone
> Finds fortunate to learn –
> When warriors hold hate in heart
> The spell will soothe their wrath.

This one is designed to calm down hotheads. Its modern equivalent would be preventing bottle fights in pubs. In northern society, which was a little like the old Wild West when it came to drawing swords, this would have been extremely useful. As would

> 9. I know a ninth: if I have need
> To shelter ship in storm,
> It quiets the wind and quells the waves,
> And soothes the sea to sleep.

which kept ships afloat and brought them to safe harbour. It

provides an instance of weather magic in a specific environment, and as the North Sea was the main adversary of any
voyage from the northern lands it was an essential for seafarers
who wanted to see home again.

> 10. I know a tenth: if ghosts should ride
> Aloft to sail the sky,
> The spell I sing sends them astray,
> Their skins and minds both lost.

The translation here is ambiguous, with some scholars citing
ghosts and others citing witches. Northern myth and magic
played a formative part in the creation of the medieval witch-
myth, and broomstick-riders spring readily to mind. There is
also an implication of shape-shifting into bird form, as skins
are lost in the process, and the spell inflicts harm that also
affects the physical body.

> 11. I know an eleventh: if to war
> Good comrades I should lead,
> The spell I chant behind my shield,
> They fight well, fare well, everywhere.

Here is another spell for protection in battle. The fact that the
spell is chanted doesn't necessarily mean it wasn't written
first, as was the case with the fourth charm. It is chanted
behind the shield, and could well form part of the back of
the shield, in the same way that a challenger inscription on
a shield boss would be a part of the shield's fabric.

> 12. I know a twelfth: if in a tree
> A corpse should hang aloft,
> Strong runes I write and stain that he
> Come down and talk with me.

This is real necromancy. Hanging was the primary method of
sacrifice to Odin, as well as a means of execution. Here we
have runes, both written and stained, to bring the victim back
to life. The medieval myth of the mandrake, which grew as a
result of the hanged man ejaculating at the moment of death

(yes, it *does* happen), could mean that these necromantic runes required staining with semen.

> 13. I know a thirteenth: if water I
> Pour over a warrior's son,
> He shall not fall in fiercest fight,
> Nor fall to slaying sword.

The act of pouring water would have been the *sending* part of this charm. It has nothing to do with baptism giving Christians an edge, otherwise Christian King Olaf the Saint wouldn't have been killed by Tore Hund at the Battle of Sticklestad in 1030. Again, this is a keep-'em-safe-in-battle charm.

> 14. I know a fourteenth men perceive
> When tales of gods I tell:
> Æsir from Elves I always know,
> As fools can never do.

Here we have an acknowledgement of the complexity of northern theology. The two families of gods were the Æsir and the Vanir, and the Vanir are frequently referred to as elves. It took an educated man or woman (such as a runemaster would have had to be) to know which was which, as most people would have a dedication to a single deity and little knowledge of any of the others, the dedication being ingrained in the family tradition rather than a matter of choice.

> 15. I know a fifteenth Thjodraerir
> Sang at Delling's door:
> Power to gods, triumph to Elves,
> And knowledge to Odin it gives.

This is an unusual charm in that our narrator (Odin) acknowledges it came from another. Thjodraerir is a dwarf who doesn't appear elsewhere in the *Elder Edda*. A literal translation of Delling is 'day-spring' or dawn. Dwarves traditionally turned to stone at dawn, and it's interesting, to say the least, that the charm is of no benefit to dwarves, giving power to the Æsir and Vanir, and to Odin, with no benefit stated as accruing to any other class of being. Yet there must be some benefit to humans. The charm bestows power, triumph and knowledge, all desired by men, and there is an implication that the power of sunlight is being harnessed in some way.

> 16. I know a sixteenth: with that spell
> Any girl grants my desires;
> The white-armed maiden's heart I turn
> Her thoughts I turn to me.

This charm is written from a male point of view, but, as Freya Aswynn has shown, can work for either sex. This is making the desired one do the right thing by your inclinations, and shows the role sexual magic, in the venereal sense, had to play in northern society. This is the charm for getting your lover.

> 17. I know a seventeenth, and if
> It's sung it has the power
> To keep the young girl true to me
> And slow to spurn my love.

And this is the charm for keeping your lover once you've used the sixteenth to get her (or him). Again, singing doesn't negate the possibility that the eight stages described above are implicit in creating the charm. It simply means that its oral recitation activated the charm. If music be the food of love . . .

> 18. I know an eighteenth never told
> To maid or wife of man;
> Save for the love held in my arms,
> Or to my sister sung.

This is the hardest of the eighteen to interpret or comment upon. The only members of the opposite sex to whom it may be told are blood siblings or committed mates. This implies it has a personal power which remains personal and powerful whilst its secrecy is maintained. Its purpose is probably to promote a personal union, either with the beloved or with other aspects of oneself. For the runemaster, living in the physical world as well as the nine worlds of northern myth to which the runes give access, this could be a way of resolving the dichotomy which life presents.

The two final verses of the *Runatál* are self-explanatory for anyone who has ever seriously considered any form of magical discipline:

> Time will it take you, Loddfafnir,
> To learn to sing these songs,
> Though helpful when you understand,
> Useful in need and knowing.

> The High One has sung this in His hall,
> Helpful to men; but giants it harms.
> Hail speaker and knower too
> Joy to those who have listened.

It is impossible in any one text to cover adequately every aspect of northern magic, but hopefully the above has given some insights into its applications and techniques as revealed by the *Runatál*. More information on its scope follows.

It has to be constantly stressed that the runes represent a highly personal system. Things that work for one won't necessarily work for another. There is no easy grimoire to dip into, which is why every magical book on the subject has its own method to promote. The best recourse, and the one I am currently endeavouring to pursue on your behalf, is to blend runic and magical finds, extant texts and known procedures, to create a thorough background for your personal system to draw upon.

THE MAGICAL TECHNIQUES OF THE NORTH

From examples found in the eddas and sagas we discover that the magic used by our northern ancestors covered an amazing range of subjects and possibilities. A brief listing of the subjects and techniques at the northern magician's disposal might run as follows:

Shape-shifting	Charms
Incantations	Prophecy and second-sight
Runic divination	Herbalism, healing and poisons
Sitting-out	Platform magic
Weather and element magic	Mind control
Evil eye	Death magic and curses
Image magic	Sexual magic
Necromancy	Ghost lore
Counter-magic	Battle magic

Many of these overlap one another, with shamanic techniques complementing herbalism and healing as an example.

The information found in the eddas and sagas has often suffered Christian overlay as it was recorded quite late from earlier oral sources. Yet it remains valid if examined carefully, yielding many valuable insights into magical techniques for anyone seeking to reconstruct its use.

SHAPE-SHIFTING

The best-known example of shape-shifting is the werewolf. A character in one of the sagas, a grandfather of a formidable runemaster, had a nickname which meant 'evening-wolf' because he was thought to change at twilight.

Several other examples of shape-shifting also occur. A wizard called Askman, cornered, tried to escape from his house by taking the shape of a boar, but was brought down by a blazing firebrand. A sorceress called Skroppa tried to conceal herself and her two foster-daughters by making them appear as first, chests of ash, and second, a sow and two piglets. Odin himself is described as being a shape-shifter in *Ynglinga Saga*. While his body lay as if asleep or dead, he'd assume the form of a bird, beast, fish or worm (serpent) and be off almost instantly to distant places.

Classic shape-shift battles are also recorded. One was between a young man and a Lappish wizard, fighting each other as dogs and then as eagles. Another battle between shape-shifters saw two neighbours, Storolf and Dufthak, fighting one another as bear and boar respectively.

Injuries to a shape-shifter often affected the human form,

as with classic werewolf lore. A witch called Thordis took walrus form and was injured in her own body when the shape was hurt.

CHARMS AND INCANTATIONS

Poetry was a powerful weapon in the northern magician's armoury, and the majority of charms and incantations were in verse. This is one area where northern magic differs radically from the reliance on long lists of names of evocation which was the stock-in-trade of the Qabalist or medieval sorcerer.

PROPHECY AND SECOND-SIGHT.

Foster-mothers were often able to touch their foster-sons before they went off to battle and predict their injuries. The future could be discovered through dreams, and the spirits of the departed could communicate with the living this way. Odin learned through magic the predestined fates of men. Weapons could also be prophetic, like a halberd which made a loud ringing sound when a man was to be killed by it, or another which dripped blood when a battle was imminent. But the greatest vehicles of prophecy were the *völvas*, such as Heidi in the poem *Völuspá*.

OTHER MAGICAL TECHNIQUES

The northern peoples had a thorough knowledge of herbalism and healing, both by herbal and amuletic applications, and were not averse to the use of natural drugs and intoxicants to produce the altered states required for some techniques.

Two powerful techniques frequently employed were platform magic and sitting-out. Sitting-out will be dealt with later (see p.122) but an appreciation of platform magic needs to be gained at this stage. The magical circle was another feature of more southerly practices which does not appear in the north. Instead there were three methods of isolating the magician from the world around him- or herself. One was the ox-hide, which was marked with nine squares and stood or sat upon.

A second was the setting out of hurdles, or lengths of wood, to form a skeletal nine square arrangement, with the centre square being occupied. The third method was the platform, literally what it says, usually supported by four posts and high enough off the ground for someone to get underneath it, which happened in at least one case where runes cut on the supports countered the ritual in progress above.

RUNE-USERS

The story of the runes isn't simply one of interpreting archaeological finds and exploring the history of language. Runes come alive when you begin to meet the people who used them, and thanks to the preservation of the eddas and sagas as part of the corpus of northern literature it's possible to do just that. It's also possible to find out exactly how runes were used magically in the past, and to go on to examine how they can be used today.

Anyone who's read *Egil's Saga* will have met the hero, Egil Skallagrimsson, and realised what an unlikely hero he is. Egil died of old age in 990, but during a long and eventful life this big, ugly man showed himself to be farmer, poet, warrior, Viking and, importantly for us, competent runemaster. He was raised by a foster-mother called Thorgerd Brak, from whom he probably learned his runes, and the first recorded instance of him using runes for magic was in 934, when he found himself at a feast on the Isle of Atley. The feast was being given by a man called Bard for the best-known Viking of all time, Erik Bloodaxe, then only a son of High King Harald Fairhair of Norway, and his new wife Gunnhild Gorm's-daughter, whose father was King of Denmark. From this it's easy to see that even in his youth Egil moved in quite high circles, despite being only the son of an Icelandic farmer whose father had a reputation as a shape-shifter.

Gunnhild was a witch who'd been trained by Lappish sorcerers, and Harald Fairhair was anti-Lapps and anti-witches, having married a woman who was both some time before. Because of this Gunnhild had to keep her magical prowess a dark secret at the time, even from her husband Erik, although he later benefitted from it when he was murdering his way through several brothers to the throne. Somehow, without speaking, she knew just by looking at Egil that this man could expose her, and she sent a poisoned cup around the table for him to drink her health with.

It wasn't the wisest of moves, as Egil suspected the gift. He cut runes on the cup, stabbed his hand, stained the runes and spoke a verse over the reddened inscription to test the contents. The cup split apart and spilled the drink harmlessly. All hell broke out and he fled the feast, killing his host Bard in the process, went into hiding and eventually escaped.

This was the beginning of a long love-hate relationship with Gunnhild. The two met and clashed magic on many more occasions, maintaining a healthy respect for one another. Egil met her again when Erik Bloodaxe was the last Viking king of Northumbria and she demanded his head. A friend interceded on the grounds of hospitality and Egil had until dawn the next day to compose a poem in honour of Erik. Gunnhild shape-shifted to interfere with the composition but was thwarted. Egil wrote the poem, known as the 'Head-Ransom', which was the first Norse poem to employ an end-rhyme, and against all odds placated Erik sufficiently to escape with his life.

Egil is recorded as having recourse to the runes in two different magical operations. The first, earlier in the story than the Head-Ransom episode, is the setting-up of a cursing pole to drive Erik and Gunnhild into their Northumbrian exile after they have cheated Egil's wife of her inheritance. The second is an incident later in his life when he is the guest of a man whose daughter is ill. Egil finds runes cut on a piece of whalebone under her bed and it turns out that a local youth has tried to cut a love charm to win her, but has cut the wrong runes. Egil scrapes off the runes, cuts new ones which he charms with a verse and stains, and the girl recovers.

POETRY AND THE RUNES

As we have seen, there was much more to using the runes for magic than just cutting the symbols. Poetry especially played an important part. It was said to be the gift of Odin, who among other things was believed to be the God of learning and inspiration. Yet the gift of poetry has strong associations with the Vanir, who almost invariably are depicted as more sensitive, feeling and artistic than the strength-pursuing Æsir. A tale is told in *Flateyjarbók* of one who slept upon the grave-mound of a dead poet to attain the gift. In this case it derived from the powers under the earth, themselves under the sway of the Vanir. This idea of obtaining gifts of inspiration or wisdom from the inhabitant of a mound even applies to Odin himself in *Völuspá*.

Odraerir, the mead of poetry, came about as a result of the truce between the Æsir and Vanir which eventually led to the combined pantheon. When the two groups of deities met to decide the peace each one spat into a vessel. From its contents a wise being called Kvasir was created, who could answer any question. Kvasir was killed by two dwarves, who mixed his blood with honey to make mead, which later came into the possession of the giant Suttung. Odin slept three nights with Suttung's daughter and persuaded her to let him have three drinks of the mead, during which he consumed it all. Flying back to the Æsir in the form of an eagle, he spat out the stolen mead into vessels they had ready, but lost a little along the way which became known as the poetaster's share. And this is how Odin and poetry came to be associated in Norse myth.

Poetry and song were vital features of any entertainments, and these songs were sung to the strains of a harp by minstrels. Sometimes they consisted of gnomic verses full of wisdom, such as can be found in sections of *Hávamál*. For companies of warriors there would be ballads of heroic or mythic deeds performed by ancestors or other members of the clan. And for variety there would be songs and poems about other clans or Germanic peoples, like that sung by one of the minstrels of Hrothgar's court as the men rode back to the hall after Beowulf's combat with Grendel.

CHARMS AND INCANTATIONS

Charms and incantations occur in a great many stories about our northern ancestors. Both were used by the witch Thurid in her effort to render the outlaw Grettir vulnerable to her foster-son, Thorbjorn Ongul. Charming a spell, whether runic or otherwise, was an important part of Norse magic, and certainly in runecraft the sequence of cutting, staining and hallowing, or charming, the runes was an inviolable practice. This was the technique used by Egil Skallagrimsson, himself a noted poet, when handed the poisoned cup at the feast on Atley Isle, and Snorri Sturluson preserved at least the spirit, if not the actual form, of the charm.

Two possible metres could have been used for charms. The first, incantation metre, was composed in the following manner. Lines one and three each had four stresses, and were divided by a caesura into two half-lines with two stresses in each. The first stressed syllable of the second half-line had to alliterate with either or both of the stresses in the first half-line. Lines two and four were not broken and contained only two or three stressed syllables, not four. Line five would be the same as line four, but with slight verbal variation in the content.

The second form was chant metre. This varied from incantation metre only in that it did not use a fifth line.

In *Anglo-Saxon Magic*, Gustav Storms demonstrates the importance which was attached to the spoken word. Expressing a command vocally was regarded as a direct means of attaining one's purpose. In the non-literate world of Norse magic, as with the Anglo-Saxons, words were believed to strengthen the power which made magic work. The form in which they were spoken would, in turn, either reinforce or weaken that power. Sung or chanted words added a strength to the spell and the role of poetry was one of the most powerful vocal forms of all, both because of the special verbal and memory skills it required, and because of the dramatic effect created when it was spoken. The word 'song' and its equivalents have been used in Indo-European (Aryan in pre-Hitler-speak) and other language groups to denote magical practices. The Lapps, the arch-sorcerers of Viking times, used the word runo to denote song or even incantation.

Once a charm had been begun it had to be completed without any form of interruption, or it might lose its effectiveness. After his fight with the giant Hrungnir, Thor had a piece of whetstone lodged in his head. The witch-wife Groa was charming this out with her incantations when the God interrupted her with news of her son. When she tried to resume the chant its efficiency had been affected by the interruption and the piece of whetstone remained lodged in Thor's forehead.

This idea of an interruption invalidating a magical practice is also found in *Kormak's Saga*, where a witch is trying to release the hero from a spell imposed by the evil Thorveig. Kormak interrupts the sacrificial rite before all the geese prepared for it have been killed, thus rendering his would-be deliverer's efforts useless.

Sound could play a part not only in the casting of spells but in their aversion as well. Leland implies that witches were obliged to pay attention to what was being spoken or sung in metre right up to its conclusion. Thus the very act of hallowing was possibly a form of counter-magic, preventing others from interfering with the spell before it was fully cast. Some charms even contain within themselves formulae designed to prevent them from being thwarted.

In the same way that sound was important, silence also played its part in magical practices, possibly being likened to the virginity prescribed for many later magical techniques. As this virginity was of purpose rather than fact, with the virgin goat intended for sacrifice quite possibly having been tupped by a ram, so silence was also of intent, implying not so much the absence of all sound but the exclusion of sounds extraneous to the practice being undertaken.

There is evidence in the eddas and sagas to show that incantations were a standard ingredient of most magical procedures. Odin uses both herbs and incantations to preserve Mimir's head from rotting and to persuade it to offer oracles as required. Odin himself is the primary teacher of incantations and charms. In *Laxdaela Saga*, Kotkel and his abominable family use incantations to raise a tempest against Thord Ingunnarsson, who has summonsed them for witchcraft. They also use incantations against Hrut Hjerolfsson, having climbed up on to his roof (platform magic?) with the effect that his youngest son, Kari, goes out during the night and is killed by their magic.

Egil Skallagrimsson used charms and incantations on several occasions. All three of his recorded uses of runecraft were accompanied by charms and his curse against Erik Bloodaxe and Gunnhild, whilst setting up the *nid-pole*, amounts to an invocation of Norway's guardian spirits to do his bidding and drive them hence.

Incantations were an important ingredient of weather magic. In *Vatnsdaela Saga*, the witch Groa accompanies her actions with a spoken formula whilst trying to bring down a landslide upon Ingimund's sons. In *Fostbroeda Saga*, Grima counters an unfavourable wind by going up on to high ground and reciting an ancient song he had been taught in childhood. Svan, in *Njal's Saga*, realizing he and his party are under magical attack, raises a concealing fog, accompanying his actions with an appropriate spoken charm.

THE POWER OF POETRY

Tradition ascribed awe and reverence to poets as well as to those who employed poetry as a part of their sorcery. The unmagical Thorleif held a grudge against Jarl Hakon after the Jarl had burned his ship. Disguised as a beggar, he penetrated the Jarl's court and recited a cursing poem before his enemy. The unfortunate Hakon was so affected by the poem that he developed a violent itch between his legs, lost his beard and most of the hair on one side of his head. The hair never grew back. Yet as well as its effect upon the Jarl, the poem also plunged the hall into darkness, made weapons clash together and caused several men to fall down dead. Hakon himself eventually, and very sensibly, fainted. Icelandic tradition held that the poem charged Hakon with a lack of virility, hence the loss of hair and the itching in areas it would have been impolite to scratch in public. Another tradition holds that certain particularly gifted poets were able to present scorn so powerful that it had a direct physical effect upon the victim.

Poetry would have been magical, apart from any other reasons, because of its strangeness. The familiar tends to be ignored because of its very familiarity. Yet anything unusual, especially that which most are unable to understand, becomes impressive by contrast. In *Vatnsdaela Saga*, Bard, preventing the storm magically created by Ulfhedin, 'spoke Irish' as a part of his counter-magic. There is a strong possibility that this phrase has nothing whatsoever to do with the Gaelic tongue, referring instead to any language or set of sounds, including rank gibberish, which would sound strange and thus be possessed of magical efficacy. Certainly there is no reason to suppose from the available evidence that the Irish were regarded as magically competent, and definitely not to the same extent as the Lapps, or even the Vikings themselves.

This idea of strangeness is reinforced by the activities of the magically proficient dwarf Mondul in *Gongu-Hrolf's Saga*. Mondul prevents the dead slain in battle from being magically resurrected to fight again. He does this by circumambulating widdershins (anti-clockwise, the opposite of 'deosil' or sun-wise) and whistling, mumbling and blowing in every direction. The sounds created take his magic out of the normal realms of magical practice, so that even if they were known to his listeners, any chants employed would have sounded new and impressive and strange because of the unusual vocal additions. In the same saga sorcerers performing platform magic were described not as chanting or reciting incantations but as making a 'dreadful noise'.

4 · THE MEANINGS OF THE RUNES

As with all scripts, the runes grew and evolved with use, taking on different meanings in different areas. The Norwegian, Icelandic and Anglo-Saxon runic poems all provide variants which, for the beginner, serve to confuse the issue rather than clarifying it. Because of this I have consistently used the (reconstructed) Common Germanic names throughout this book.

While the role played by the runic poems must, because of their comparatively late dates, be suspect when attempting to consider the earliest assigned meanings of the rune-names, they served a useful mnemonic role at the time of their composition. In all probability there was a poem which gave the names of the Common Germanic Futhark, but it would have been too early, or too secret in later times, to have been recorded.

INTERPRETATIONS OF THE RUNES

As we have seen, each rune possesses at least one meaning linking it to an idea or object. With many of the runes there are at least two or three possible meanings.

ᚠ FEHU The meaning of this rune is 'cattle', a vital aspect of the life of any agricultural community and an important factor in the economy of a group of peoples initially unacquainted with the use of money. The rune represents possessions won or earned and thus also material gain.

The Anglo-Saxon runic poem describes wealth as a comfort to all men, then goes on to add that they must bestow it freely if they wish to gain favour in the sight of the Lord. This is not the Christian interpolation that it at first appears, as the bestowing of rewards and generosity is an important feature of much of the extant saga literature. As we shall see later there is even a 'gift' rune.

The Norwegian and Icelandic rune poems take a more cynical view and regard wealth as a cause of discord among kinsmen. The Norwegian poem (NRP) compares this to the wolf living in the forest, whilst the 'fire of the sea and path of the grave-fish' of the Icelandic text (IRP) is a clear allusion to its inspiration of Viking practices.

The rune may be linked to Frey or Freya. Oxen were sacrificed to Frey, as detailed in *Gisli's Saga* and *Viga-Glum's Saga*. IRP glosses 'gold' for this rune and both gold and amber, which was mentioned by Tacitus as one of the trade commodities of the Aestii which fetched a good price from the Romans, are referred to in Norse myth as the 'tears of Freya'. Significantly the Aestii were said to have worshipped the mother of the gods and worn her emblem, the wild boar. This will later be found linked to Frey, Freya's brother, and while in later myth Freya tends to be the whore of the gods rather than their mother she has also been identified with Frigg.

The necklace Brisingamen, obtained by Freya at the price of sleeping with the four dwarf craftsmen who created it, is the symbol of Freya's wealth. The rich God Njord, her father, has been implied here, but his place comes more properly when we examine *Laguz*.

Runes, as both letters and mnemonic symbols, undoubtedly had correspondences attached to them. Continuing the association of *Fehu* with Freya, the following correspondences should be mentioned. Freya found her missing husband, Od, beneath a myrtle tree. Myrtle wreaths are said to have been worn by northern brides, possibly as a symbol of the defloration of the first night.

The butterfly was called Freya's hen. Cats were sacred to Freya and drew her chariot. The cat isn't a particularly old domestic animal in Scandinavia, and a suggestion has been made that the creatures which pulled the chariot may have been ermine. These could also have provided the white catskin gloves for the *völva* in *Eirik the Red's Saga*. The main qualification for an animal being designated *köttr*, a cat, was the ability shared by both cats and ermine to catch mice.

With the advent of Christianity all the Norse gods were demoted to the status of common demons and Freya became the patroness of the witches. Her sacred animal, the cat, became the archetypal witch's familiar, or animal go-between serving both the Christian devil and herself. Two of her sacred birds, the swallow and the cuckoo, also fell from grace.

An identification of Norse paganism with later witchcraft isn't as fanciful as might at first appear. Several authors have already made the identification, and witch persecutions were chiefly a Northern European phenomenon.

When speaking of Nerthus, who might be identified as a mother of the gods, Tacitus mentions that her carriage was drawn by kine. Two of Freya's titles are *hörn* and *syr*, the former meaning liquid manure and the latter meaning sow. Both have, albeit differing, fertility connections, and sow would be an appropriate attribute in opposition to Frey's boar.

Fehu is pronounced as F in modern English.

ᚢ URUZ   This represents the aurochs, the great wild and untameable cattle of northern Europe which are now extinct. Julius Caesar described them in *De Bello Gallico* as slightly less than the elephant in size and of the colour and shape of a bull. They had extraordinary strength and speed and were exceptionally ferocious. By far the best way of capturing an aurochs was with a pit trap, and the proof of the adventure was the display of the dead beast's horns. These were of massive size

and were bound at the tips with silver for use as
festive cups.

Thus the aurochs came to be a symbol of great strength and
speed, and in being such a challenge to the hunter, also a
symbol of man's prowess. There was also a parallel to be
implied in its defence against the hunter, which compared to
man defending his home against the invader. The Anglo-Saxon
rune poem (ASRP) describes the beast in terms similar to those
employed by Caesar, as both proud and 'having great horns; it
is a very savage beast and fights with its horns; a great ranger of
the moors, it is a creature of mettle'. NRP took a new meaning
of dross, or slag, while perplexingly offering the line that the
'reindeer often races over the frozen snow'. This echoes the
speed of the aurochs and shows an awareness, albeit a reduced
one, of the earlier meaning. IRP offered a meaning of shower,
making the strength of the noble beast into the force of rain
beating down upon crops and livestock.

The bull was believed to have been dedicated to Thor,
and certainly the strength of the one reinforces a possible
correspondence with the other. 'Achievement' may also have
been a meaning of this rune, with the hunting of the aurochs
providing an ultimate test of strength and initiative.

Uruz is pronounced as the double O sound in the modern
English word 'book'.

ThURISAZ   This is of disputed meaning, but is generally regarded as unpleasant in nature. Giant, troll and
demon have all been given as possible interpretations,
and the 'thorn' of ASRP cannot be ignored either.

This is the troll-rune as used in the Norse poem *For Scirnis*
or *Skirnir's Ride*. It has the power when employed in a
sequence of three to alter the meanings of succeeding runes.
Its use was said to evoke demons from the underworld, and it
was also known as 'Hrungnir's heart', after the legend recorded
by Snorri Sturluson of the killing of the giant Hrungnir by
Thor. The giant's heart was said to be like the runic character,
sharp-edged and three-cornered, and on the Skane bracteate
1 *Thurisaz* is written ▷ , which is perfectly in accord with
this description.

ASRP reads 'thorn' for the meaning of this rune. This description of a sharp and evil thing to touch, uncommonly severe to those who sit amongst them, applies as well to the enemies of the Æsir as to thorns. NRP and IRP retain 'giant' as the meaning, and ascribe to these creatures a penchant for torturing women. This could well be a sexual allusion, as the ideas of the thorn and the penis are not unrelated, as the archaic but still current slang term 'prick', meaning the male member, ably demonstrates.

The shape-shifting power of this rune is that ascribed to trolls or ogres. That it is hardly favourable is supported by the NRP gloss that 'misfortune makes few men cheerful'.

Thurisaz is pronounced th as in 'thin'.

ANSUZ   This rune has the meaning of a god or deity, specifically one of the Æsir, and as such it is usually ascribed to Odin as their leader. In later times Odin was also regarded as a wind God and the leader of the Wild Hunt of disembodied and damned souls, leading them through the air on the storm clouds. The hanged were sacred to him because of his hanging upon Yggdrasil to win the runes, and sacrifice to Odin by hanging was occasionally practised.

ASRP terms this rune *Os*, praising it as the source of all language, a blessing and joy and a comfort to the wise. NRP reads *Oss*, meaning an estuary and further describing it as the beginning of most (Viking) voyages. A further cryptic gloss is that a 'scabbard is of swords'. IRP reads *Oss* as god, specifically making the God Odin by adding 'Prince of Asgard and Lord of Valhalla'. In case this were insufficient to render the meaning clear, the Latin gloss in IRP is 'Jupiter, Father of the Gods', which Odin indubitably was – physically in most cases.

ASRP also provides a verse for *Aesc*, the 'ae' rune of the Anglo-Saxon Futhork, which would have taken the place of *Ansuz* had not *Oss* been ascribed. The meaning equated here is the ash tree, said to be exceedingly high and precious to men, whose sturdy trunk offers a stubborn resistance though attacked by many. The ash is the worldly counterpart of the world-tree Yggdrasil, and this meaning reinforces the connection of the A-rune with Odin/God. Indeed, Yggdrasil means 'Ygg's horse' as 'Ygg's gallows', and it was here that Odin hung while discovering the runes, making ash one of the sacred trees of both runecraft and Northern myth. According to one authority venomous animals wouldn't shelter beneath its branches. A carriage with axles of ash went faster and tools with ash handles performed better for the craftsman. Witches rode upon ash branches and ash is the ideal handle for a besom. Those who ate the red buds of the tree upon St John's Eve would be invulnerable to bewitchment.

Yggdrasil is rendered as Ygg's, or Odin's, horse or gallows. As the discoverer of the runes, Odin was also the sorcerer of the gods, and his magic is invariably more powerful than anyone else's. Among his most famous worshippers was the runemaster Egil Skallagrimsson.

The spear was pre-eminently Odin's weapon and ash was the wood most favoured for spear-shafts. The casket in which Idun kept the apples which prevented the gods from ageing was made of ash-wood.

Ansuz is pronounced as in the modern English word 'stack'.

R RAIDO   A variety of meanings have been ascribed to this rune. They include journey, cartwheel, ride, long journey on horseback and cart or chariot. The rune could have served as a journey charm to protect both the living and the dead, and there is also some reason for ascribing it to the God Thor. The Old Norse word reid could mean either a wheeled vehicle or thunder. Thunder was caused by Thor's wheeled chariot drawn by two he-goats, rattling across the sky.

ASRP offers Rad as the name for the rune, but in doing so fails to provide a clear meaning. The gloss, that Rad seems 'easy to a warrior indoors and very courageous to one abroad on horseback', fits well with meanings of either thunder or riding. Both NRP and IRP take riding as the meaning, IRP in its Latin gloss adding iter, or journey. NRP is again somewhat cryptic in its remark that Regin, the master-smith who was foster-father of Sigurd and brother of the dragon Fafnir, forged the finest sword.

Thor is closely associated with the oak, and it is widely recognized that the god of the oak, the tree more frequently struck by lightning than any other, is also the god of thunder. ASRP provides a verse for *Ac*, the 'ai' rune, describing how acorns fatten swine for man's table, as well as the wood being used for building ships. Oak was also the wood of the Yule log, and it would have been very appropriate for the wood burned upon Thor's principal festival to come from his sacred tree. Oak pillars are associated with Thor in Iceland, as in *Eyrbyggja Saga*, where Thorolf Mostur-Beard throws his high seat pillars, made of oak, overboard to establish where he should settle, the decision being taken for him by the place at which they drift to land. Here, as is other places, the additional matter which can be derived from the extra verses provided by ASRP invariably seems to show that, in order to find material with which to gloss the extra letters, an earlier, now lost, source was dissected.

This rune is pronounced exactly as in modern English.

KAUNAZ As with *Raido*, no immediate and clear interpretation emerges for this rune. Meanings which have been given include torch, light, boil, abscess and ulcer. ASRP reads 'torch', known to all living by its pale, bright flame, and adding that it always burns where princes sit within. This could read just as easily if the meaning were fever, and the less equivocal renderings of IRP and NRP agree that the rune's most likely interpretation is an association with some form of discomfort or disease. Both these texts take ulcer as the most probable meaning, and IRP's 'disease fatal to children, and painful spot, and abode of mortification' can leave us in little doubt, as does its Latin gloss of *flagella*. NRP provides a direct parallel with ASRP by stating that this rune 'makes a man pale'.

Other possible interpretations include an association with cremation, as well as a correspondence with *kano*, skiff, the sacred vehicle of the cult of Nerthus. Some form of burning pain or fever, however, still seems the most likely interpretation.

The rune is pronounced exactly as in modern English.

X GEBO   This rune has the meaning of a gift, but the nature of the gift remains ambiguous. It could be the sacrifice of man giving to the gods, or the bounty of the gods giving to man. Man giving to the gods would imply a religious act, and religion could be regarded as the gift of the gods to man.

This rune was said to protect against the poisoned cup, and as such may have formed a part of the sequence scored by Egil Skallagrimsson at Bard's feast, when Gunnhild passed a poisoned cup to him. When we examine the numerology of runecraft later we shall see that three is an important number, and beer-barrels marked with three Xs, or gebo-runes, are almost a cliché.

This was one of the runes which was dropped from the later Scandinavian Futhork, and only ASRP holds a comment upon it. The name as given here is *Gyfu*, and it translates to mean generosity. Thus it is said to bring credit and honour to the support of one's dignity, and in the sense of charity it furnishes help and subsistence to those in need. Again this represents situations applicable to man to man, man to god or god to man.

The pronunciation of this rune is rather difficult. It is only rarely used as a hard sound, as in 'girl', and never as a J equivalent. Mostly it was a soft sound with the tongue further back on the palate than for the hard sound, producing a longer, more rolling 'gh'.

P WUNJO   The meaning of this rune was bliss, comfort and even glory. It might be taken to mean the support of concrete possessions, but it primarily represented an absence of suffering. Linguistically it compares favourably with the Germanic *wulthuz*, glory and *winjo*, pasture, both of which support its meaning. *Wulthuz* may also support an association with the Norse God Ull.

ASRP has *Wenne*, bliss, enjoyed by the prosperous and contented ones who don't know suffering, sorrow or anxiety. One opinion has it that this rune induces intoxication, linking it to the Gothic *woths*, furious or raging, and the frenzy rune which was employed by Skirnir. *Woths* may in turn descend from the Germanic *wod*-z, which has the same meaning and is one of the most probable derivations of Odin. In the Anglo-Saxon 'Nine Herbs Charm' Odin performs magic with 'glory wands', leading us around in almost a complete circle, with the truth lying somewhere therein. After all, there is no reason why the 'glory wands' should not be 'glory staves', which in turn would relate to the 'glory runes' of *Wunjo*. The nine twigs bore the runic initials of the nine plants they represented, which in turn were related to the powers inherent in the plants.

This rune is pronounced as in modern English.

H HAGALAZ   This rune means 'hail', both as an aspect of the weather and in the sense of a hail of missiles in battle. In both senses it has the implication of a destructive and order-threatening force.

ASRP describes hail as the 'whitest of grain, whirled from the vault of the heavens and tossed about by wind before turning finally to water'. NRP agrees with this, whilst irrelevantly adding that Christ created the world of old. IRP refers specifically to hail as an aspect of the weather, with its 'cold grain and shower of sleet and sickness of serpents'. 'Sickness of serpents' is a kenning, or poetic simile, for Winter.

Both as a weather weapon and as a phenomenon of battle, hail represents a force not completely within an individual's control.

The flaming wheels, which were later representations of symbols from the *hällristningar*, traditionally rolled by the Germanic peoples upon St John's Eve, were called 'hail-wheels'. Their purpose, in that uncertain climate, was to protect the ripening crops from the ravages of hail. This opens the speculation that the power of this rune could be magically counteracted by the use of the sun-wheel. Another measure against hail is remarkable because it was employed by a Christian bishop yet obviously referred back to paganism in its usage. The dignitary concerned took a piece of wax from the grave of a saint and cut pagan signs, which were most likely runes, upon it. This piece of wax was then fastened to a tall tree to ward off the hailstorms which had previously damaged the bishop's crops.

This rune is pronounced as in modern English.

NAUTHIZ   This rune has the meanings of need, constraint and even, in extremis, misery. Some authorities read this as a fate-rune and equate it with the *Nornir*, or Fates, of Norse myth. It had the power of providing help when scratched upon a fingernail, and its meaning thus vacillates between assistance and the need to survive.

While *Nauthiz* might provide assistance, NRP glibly states that constraint gives scant choice, and that a naked man will be chilled by the frost. IRP also offers constraint, but equates the rune with the need for work, thereby offering a solution to its attendant difficulties. It glosses the rune with the Latin *opera*, or work, confirming this. ASRP alone offers a degree of hope, despite rendering the rune-name as *Nyd*, which translates as trouble.

The rune is pronounced as in modern English.

ISA   This means ice, which, like hail, is an essentially damaging natural force. ASRP regards ice as very cold and slippery, like a floor which has been made from glass but which is nevertheless fair to look at. NRP calls it the broad bridge and adds that the blind man must be led. This could be taken either as a cryptic warning or as a straightforward piece of practical advice.

IRP glosses this rune with the Latin *glacies*, or ice, and provides kennings with the phrases 'bark of rivers', 'destruction of the doomed' and 'roof of the wave', despite the fact that salt water freezes with less ease than fresh.

In some interpretations of the story of Odin's wooing of Rind, ice is regarded as the power he used to bind his enchanted bride-to-be. If this is the case, then one virtue of this rune might be to reinforce the strength of a rune-spell.

The rune is pronounced as in modern English.

ᛃ JERA Interpretations which have been offered for this rune include year, spear, harvest, year of plenty and year of good harvest.

Both NRP and IRP prefer to render the meaning as 'plenty', IRP adding a good summer and thriving crops for good measure. NRP, cryptic as ever, adds that the peace-loving Danish king Frothi was generous, adding to the overall impression of prosperity associated with this rune. IRP offers the Latin gloss *annus*, year, and ASRP reads 'summer' while giving the name of the rune as *Ger*. This derives from *gear*, a word originally referring to the warm part of the year.

The concepts of a season of fertility and a good harvest were vital, in the true meaning of 'vital', to agricultural communities in the uncertain northlands.

The rune is pronounced as in the modern English word 'yes'.

ᛇ EIHWAZ This rune means 'yew', a wood both sacred to runecraft and used for the making of bows. The hunting God Ull built his hall in *Ydalir*, Yewdale, and the bow was regarded as his sacred weapon.

ASRP and NRP eulogize the qualities of the tree, which has rough bark, stands hard and fast in the earth, is a guardian of flame, a joy upon an estate, the greenest of trees in winter and, lastly, apt to crackle when it burns. Only IRP reads 'bow', describing it as an implement of battle and speeder of the arrow, and using *arcus*, bow, for the Latin gloss. In Christian times Ull's place was taken by St Hubert, the hunter, patron of the first month of the year. Ull was regarded as a winter God and the first month began, appropriately, on 22nd November, when the sun passed into the sign of Sagittarius, the archer.

In Christian myth, the yew was both a help and a hindrance to witches. According to some, it was of assistance because it was planted near to churches, thus offering some sacrilegious but unspecified benefit. According to others it protected churchyards from the demonic arts of these vile creatures. Certainly it was of use to the third witch in *Macbeth*, who employed among other charm ingredients 'slips of yew, sliver'd in the moon's eclipse.' In German folklore, yew ground to powder and baked was a sovereign remedy against the bite of a mad dog.

The rune is pronounced as in modern English 'yet'.

PERTHO Perhaps the greatest mystery in the futhark is the meaning of this rune. Attempts to interpret its meaning range from dance, through fruit tree, to hearth. ASRP offers 'chessman' as a meaning, describing it as a source of recreation and amusement to the great gathered together in the banqueting hall. Yet in citing this, Dickins notes a comparison of the rune-name with the Slavonic word *pizda*, or vulva. This would make the rune sacred to Frigg as the mother figure of the gods and provide a direct parallel with the essentially male fertility implicit in the later rune *Inguz*. *Pertho* has also been thought to be symbolic of the magical powers of the earth, through a supposed derivation from the Latin *petra*, rock.

A brief examination of some of the other meanings may serve to clear things up somewhat. Dance was one of the earliest symbolic acts of worship, possibly because of the erotic excitation it was capable of producing. Certainly in some of its motions it could provide parallels with movements used in sexual activity. Its suppression by Christianity, probably during the council held under Boniface in 742, and the identification in Anglo-Saxon of the word *lâc* with both religious ceremony and dance, combine unerringly when we realize that *lâc* forms the second syllable of the Anglo-Saxon for wedlock, and is still identifiable in the word we use today.

A possible candidate for the fruit tree might well be the elder. 'Devil's wood' is a folk-name still extant for elder in our own time, because of its difficult properties when burning. Elder is a wood associated with witchcraft, and its name is said to be derived from the Slavonic *hohl*, hollow, itself a synonym for the female genitalia. The use of both elder flowers and berries for wine, Odin's intoxicating staple diet, is well-known. The church's regard for witchcraft as an essentially female phenomenon, coupled with 'devil's wood', and the derivation of its name from a synonym for the female sexual organs, begins to reinforce the interpretation of vulva for this rune. Elder is regularly used in charms to relieve pain, and the therapeutic value of sexual intercourse is too widely known to require more comment.

The rune is pronounced as in modern English.

ALGIZ   This rune implies defence and protection, possibly even in the form of an amulet or temple sanctuary, and related words are the Gothic *alhs*, temple and the Old English *ealgian*, to protect. There may also be a relationship here with the mysterious runeword *alu*. The meaning has also been equated with the elk, mentioned by Caesar as sleeping upright leaning against a tree to elude the hunter more easily, and thus in some measure a symbol of preservation in the face of adversity.

ASRP confusingly takes the meaning as some kind of sedge-grass found in marshes, and inflicting terrible wounds on anyone incautious enough to brush against it. This would be an admirable protection against being uprooted or eaten.

The rune's resemblance to the outstretched hand, palm outwards or upwards, has also been pointed out by some writers, again implying a protective power which can avert or banish evil. This is a tempting reinforcement of the rune's meaning, but it has the disadvantage of leading into the highly speculative area of attributing pictographic meanings to the runes. This has led many would-be interpreters into gross errors, yet its resemblance to the branch configurations of ash, walnut or linden trees, at which witches were wont to assemble at the full moon in Slavonian gypsy lore, might be noted in passing.

The rune is pronounced somewhere between z and r.

SOWULO   This rune represents the sun, the heavenly body upon which all life depends and one of the principal objects of any ancient worship. Caesar observed that the Germani worshipped both the sun and the moon, and both of these luminaries would have played an important part in daily life, regulating as they do between them both the seasons and the tides.

ASRP describes this rune as the hope of seafarers, NRP

has it as the light of the world, and IRP poetically calls it shield of the clouds, shining ray and either destroyer of ice or circling wheel. The Latin gloss is *rota*, wheel. As shining is the most frequently applied adjective to the sun we may trace a correspondence with the Shining God of Norse myth — Baldur, patron of innocence and light. Camomile was called 'Baldur's brow' because the flower was so immaculately pure it resembled the god's forehead. Baldur is also closely associated with the mistletoe, a shaft of which was set into blind Hodur's hand by Loki to kill Baldur.

The rune is pronounced as in modern English 'sea'.

↑ TEIWAZ This is the rune of Tyr, God of war, giver of victory and protector from harm. Amuletic use of this rune was widespread, even in the earlier centuries of runecraft.

ASRP stands alone in not ascribing the rune to the God of war. Yet although it prefers to make Tyr a star, possibly a circumpolar constellation, the descriptive gloss goes well enough with the war God: 'well does it keep faith with princes; it is ever on its course over the mists of night and never fails.' Thus it confirms the sense of optimism integral to this rune.

NRP and IRP, which glosses Tyr as Mars, both refer to Tyr as the one-handed God. When the Fenris Wolf was being bound with the fetter from which it could not escape, Tyr placed his hand in the creature's mouth as a false pledge. It discovered it was trapped and bit Tyr's right hand off. Despite the falsity of the pledge, this story is used to illustrate Tyr's nobility of spirit. Frey gave his sword for love of Gerd; Odin gave his eye for personal love of wisdom; but Tyr gave his hand for love of his fellows. (For this reason the wrist is referred to as the 'wolf-joint'.)

Aconite was known in the north as 'Tyr's helm', an interesting fact in view of its folk name of wolfsbane. Wolfsbane was also known as Sagittarius because its poison was used on arrow-heads. It was also a principal ingredient of the witches' flying ointments. In view of the rune being a perfect representation of an arrow, this association is both remarkable and apposite.

This rune has also been identified as the *geir's-odd* or spear-rune. This was the sign supposed to be cut by an ageing warrior in his own flesh so that he might enter Valhalla, instead of dying a 'straw-death' in bed of old age.

Teiwaz is the commonest of the runic symbols found upon English cremation urns. On the one from Sawston in Yorkshire, it appears in connection with that other archetypal Germanic symbol the swastika.

The rune is pronounced as in modern English.

ʙ BERKANA   The birch tree was regarded as sacred and associated with spring fertility rites. Idun was believed to be the Goddess of spring, and her youth, vigour and beauty were symbolic of the vegetative resurrection which the season brought. She was also the keeper of the apples that gave perpetual and spring-like youth to the gods.

ASRP confuses the issue by describing a tree which is more likely to be a poplar than a birch. NRP and IRP agree that

Figure 6. The cremation urn found at Sawston in Yorkshire

66

birch has the greenest leaves of any shrub, and NRP comments cryptically that Loki was fortunate in his deceit, which would appear more perfectly applicable to the mistletoe.

This rune is rarely pronounced as a stop, as in 'bird'. Elliott compares the sound to that made when blowing out a candle without rounding the lips.

MEHWAZ This is the horse rune. Horses have been regarded as sacred since the earliest times, and Tacitus describes pure white horses, kept at public expense and not used for any kind of work, yoked to a chariot and used to confirm divinations by their snorts and neighs, which were interpreted either by the king or by a state priest. He added that the horses were believed to be privy to the counsels of the gods. Odin's own eight-legged mount, Sleipnir, was believed to have been either pure white or dappled grey.

ASRP confirms the rune-meaning of horse, describing it as a joy to princes in the presence of warriors, a steed in the pride of its hoofs when rich men bandy words about it, and ever a source of comfort to the restless. The horse was frequently regarded as sacred to Frey, and the animal's dedication to that deity is a central theme of *Hrafnkel's Saga*.

The heathen Swedes were called 'horse-eaters' by their converted compatriots, an appellation which continued to be used throughout the eleventh and twelfth centuries. Such a diet, albeit ceremonial, was also the reputed provender of giants and witches and was associated with the worship of Odin. The witches, the equivalent of the old pagan *völvas* or sybils, suitably denigrated for the purposes of the Christian hierarchy, were well-suited to keep company with the giants, who were themselves a distorted memory of the old pagan heroes. The horse was the favoured animal of that folkloric archetype the solar hero, and thus to the virtue of this rune may be added that certainty which accompanied the exploits of the invulnerable hero carried along by the sacred solar horse.

The rune is pronounced as in modern English 'end'.

M MANNAZ   This rune stands for man, either the individual or the race, and it was thought to possess powers for defence and protection.

ASRP comments with true pessimism that every man is doomed to fail his fellows, since the Lord by his decree will commit the vile carrion to the earth. NRP adds, cryptically as ever, that great is the claw of the hawk. IRP maintains a steady optimism by describing man as the augmentation of the earth and the adornment of ships, and glosses the Latin *homo*, man. Some authorities note mention in Tacitus of an earth-born God called Tuisto, who had a son called Mannus, thus establishing a speculative link between the deity and this rune.

The rune is pronounced as in modern English.

L LAGUZ   This rune represents water, perhaps as a source of fertility. One authority regards the name as a late replacement and prefers to read an earlier sense of leek, or herb, pointing to an association of the shape of the leek with pagan phallic practices. Whilst this coincides with the fertility aspect of the rune, the water interpretation is very well established, and the rune is associated with the Vanir God Njord. The marine sponge was known as 'Njord's glove', and he was regarded as a wealthy deity associated with the sea. Gulls and seals were sacred to him.

ASRP reads 'ocean' for the meaning and glosses this with a note on the terrors of the deep. NRP reads waterfall, but glosses Njord's richness with the line that 'ornaments are of gold'. IRP glosses the Latin *lacus*, lake, and confirms water as the eddying stream and the land of the fish and the broad geyser.

The rune is pronounced as in modern English.

◇ INGUZ   This rune is associated with the deity Frey, also known as the hero Ing. It denotes fertility, and as Frey has been represented ithyphallically, it may well stand for the male generative organ and be a direct equivalent to the female *Pertho*.

ASRP refers to Ing as a departed hero of the Danes. Fertility flourishes best in peacetime and Frey's cult as a god of peace and prosperity descends from that of the earlier Goddess Nerthus. The *jul*, or Yule, feast was dedicated to Frey, and the head of his sacred animal, the boar, was served crowned with laurel and rosemary.

The rune is pronounced as in the modern English word 'singer'.

OTHILA   This rune means inheritance, in the wide sense of anything of value which can be passed down or handed over, including knowledge. It can also refer to the ancestral home and, by extension, the native land. This is one of the runes not included in IRP and NRP, and so we only have the words of ASRP to work with for amplification. ASRP glosses the meaning with 'estate', which is very dear to every man if he is able to enjoy, in his own home, whatever is right and proper in constant prosperity. Unfortunately here we have the materialistic tendencies of medieval Christianity creeping in to modify the wider meaning.

The rune is pronounced as in modern English.

DAGAZ   This stands for day, the security of daylight as opposed to the inconvenience, if not actual terror, of night. Day is the time of being able to see and thus counteract one's foes, the time when work may go ahead well. Again, we only have the glosses from ASRP to help augment the interpretation here. Yet the poem is optimistic, for once, if Christian, in saying that the glorious light of the Creator, sent by the Lord, is beloved of men, serviceable to all, and a source of hope and happiness to both rich and poor alike.

Despite representing the letter D this rune is usually pronounced 'th' as in modern English 'then'.

5 · USES OF THE RUNES

USES OF SINGLE RUNES

Single runes stand both for the meaning of their names and for the powers associated with them. One of the best examples is *Teiwaz*, which represents both the name and the powers of the God Tyr. It was frequently inscribed to invoke his aid in obtaining victory in battle and has been found upon a number of weapons. One example of its use is on a late sixth/early seventh century sword pommel from Faversham in Kent. On each of its two sides, the *Teiwaz* rune set between two vertical lines has been engraved and blackened with niello. An instruction regarding the use of this rune can be found in the *Sigrdrifomál*.

> Triumph runes, if you desire,
> You'll etch on hilt of sword,
> Some on the sheath, some on the blade,
> And call out twice on Tyr.

Examples of other runes being used in the same way, standing for the name-word or powers associated with it, aren't hard to find. The Skodberg bracteate uses *Jera* to signify 'good harvest'. *Fehu* appears on the Floksand scraper to denote prosperity, and is similarly used on the Femo bracteate. *Raido* is often used in inscriptions as shorthand for 'rune', as it is on the

Wapno and Sievern bracteates, both dated to around 450. The Thorsberg shield-boss, around the same date, uses *Hagalaz* to denote hail.

A tenth century Swedish inscription from Ingoldstat has the old *Dagaz* rune standing for its name in a fascinating position – right in the middle of the Younger Futhork. At least one authority has concluded that this indicates the idiographic use of runes to have been known before the futhark reduced from twenty-four to sixteen letters. It also argues well for individual runes possessing individual powers, and by inference for the magical power of seemingly unintelligible sequences in the Common Germanic Futhark.

USES OF RUNE SEQUENCES

The most overtly puzzling use of runes is to be found in extant mysterious sequences which are incapable of philological or other interpretation without a knowledge of the runic numerology which we will explore later. Examples are found on such diverse items as the Lindholm amulet, the Gummarp stone with its three *Fehu* runes denoting great wealth, and the Ellstad stone with its mysterious multiple use of *Isa* and *Kaunaz*. The Rök stone in Ostergotland bears the longest runic inscription in Scandinavia, containing about 725 characters which include both cryptic runes and numerological sequences. Its interpretation isn't helped by the fact that more than one futhark is used on its two faces.

The Gorlev stone, dating from around 800, contains both a futhark and a mysterious rune sequence as well as an intelligible inscription. Einar Haugen renders it as 'Thjodvi raised this stone for Odinkar – Younger Futhark – Enjoy your memorial well. th m k iii sss ttt iii lll. I set the runes rightly. Gunni, Armundr . . .' Haugen converts the underlined sequence into thistill mistill kistill and suggests that it has some magical importance.

USES OF THE WHOLE FUTHARK

The Thames scramaseax is a short sword which bears a
complete futhark as well as what is probably the name
of its owner. It is from the entire futhark being graven on
various objects that the order of the runes is known. There
is no easy, or readily-apparent, answer as to where and
why the entire futhark should be chosen for engraving, for
it appears in a variety of places. The Thames scramaseax
is undoubtedly a weapon, but the futhark is also found
on jewellery and other artefacts, such as the sixth century

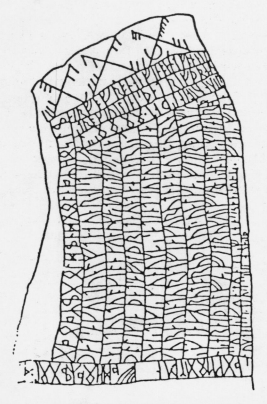

Figure 7. The Rök Stone

Grumpan and Vadstena bracteates, the Kylver stone, the Breza marble column, the Charnay clasp and the Lindkaer and Overhornbaek bracteates.

Runes and the dead

In the case of the Kylver stone, it was never intended that the futhark should be seen by anyone living, as the slab formed one side of a fourth century Gotland grave. Obviously the dead alone were intended to benefit from its power, and perhaps the inscription was designed to let the deceased know that rueful consequences from still living runemasters might attend any return from the nether-world.

An alternative, in view of the practice of placing runes beneath the deceased's tongue to assist his answers before Odin at the lower-world thingstead, could be that the inscription is there to assist the deceased. An inscription found beneath a grave slab from Eggjum states that the runes weren't cut with an iron knife and neither stone nor runes had ever been exposed to sunlight. Thus both stone and inscription, kept in darkness until their discovery centuries later, had been dedicated to the service of the deceased. That the inscribed side had been turned towards the corpse reinforces the argument that they were intended to have some influence upon him.

The Kylver stone's fir tree like symbol, following the futhark,

Figure 8. Symbols on the Kylver stone

73

consists of one vertical stave with six branches to the left and eight to the right. Authorities differ as to its interpretation. Some believe it a magically-reinforced *Teiwaz*, which is unlikely unless two strokes on the left have been lost. Others regard it as non-runic altogether. A third alternative is that it is a coded rune of some kind.

Like the Eggjum and Kylver stones, the sixth century Noleby stone was also intended to be placed within a grave, reinforcing the opinion that, if they served the living, it was by influencing the dead. These examples show that the practice of cutting stones to lie with the dead in their graves was a well-established magical feature of the times. The Noleby, Kylver and Eggjum inscriptions cover 500 years between them, and while they may be significant examples, they are not to be regarded as unique. Musset remarks that the practice was also known to the Etruscans and the Graeco-Romans.

PALINDROMES

One of the Kylver stone's mysteries is the placing of the palindrome *sueus* after the futhark. Perhaps here there is a similarity of intent to the scattering of beans about the graves of suspected Central European revenants, a practice designed to trap them into counting the beans and thereby prevent them from wandering forth to plague the living. The revenant would seek the end of the palindrome and, being led back to its beginning, and so on, be confined to nether-Hel. Leland believes that the distinctive interlocking patterns of Viking art were believed to bring good luck and avert evil influence in the same way, constraining witches and other malevolents to follow the patterns to their end and thus be diverted from their evil purpose.

However, there are other possible interpretations. Palindromes appear to have been associated with the dead but only a limited number of examples are available for study. The ascription of all that is imperfectly understood to religious or magical usage, and let us not forget that the cult of the dead was a part of this, is a favoured escape for the uncertain scholar.

As a word, *sueus* has no apparent meaning. But, as we've

already seen, runes aren't just used to build words. If *sueus* is taken as a sequence of five individual runes instead of as a word, a cyclical formula can be derived which is neither totally meaningless nor easily dismissable:

SOWULO	URUZ	EHWAZ	URUZ	SOWULO
sun	strength	confirms	strength	sun

The only non-traditional interpretation used above is that for *Ehwaz*, usually read as 'horse'. Even with the original meaning there is sense to be made, for the horse was an acknowledged solar animal. Tacitus states in the *Germania* that the sacred white horses were used to confirm a divination by lot (runes), and it is therefore not such a giant leap to read *Ehwaz* as meaning 'confirmation'. The palindrome thus becomes 'The sun's strength confirms the strength of the sun.' This isn't so very different from the old saw that 'a man should be judged by his actions', and before it is dismissed as isolated gibberish another example should be examined.

A wooden stave from a grave-mound at Froslov in South Jutland bears six characters set between points, of which the first may not be runic. The remaining five, however, form the palindrome *ziliz*, which again has no meaning as a word. As a palindrome it renders:

ALGIZ	ISA	LAGUZ	ISA	ALGIZ
protection	ice	water	ice	protection

– which is to say 'Ice protects water and water protects ice.' Again this could be taken for gibberish, but there is a mystery here to be revealed, with a little more persistence.

Both the *sueus* and *ziliz* palindromes enshrine information about natural forces, and neither is in itself completely illogical. Thus the palindrome combines the advantages of a proverb with an unusual and striking mnemonic formula which makes it of service to both the living and the dead. Pausing to take an item of later evidence, the SATOR square, we find the central line and axis of the twenty-five letters to read *tenet*. Again, in runic form this will give us:

| TEIWAZ | EHWAZ | NAUTHIZ | EHWAZ | TEIWAZ |
| victory | confirms | need | confirms | victory |

– and as a palindromic sequence, like *sueus* and *ziliz* the idea of victory resulting from need and need desiring victory is far from nonsensical.

The SATOR square shows up in Anglo-Saxon charms and, albeit at a late date, entered the runic tradition as well, having

Figure 9. The SATOR square

been found among the runic discoveries at Bryggen which date from the thirteenth century. The full SATOR formula uses the letters of PATER NOSTER, reminding us of the runic Paternoster in the *Dialogue of Solomon and Saturnus*. This association becomes irresistible in view of three late Swedish names for the SATOR square:

Fans fyrkant	– the Devil's square
Djavulens Latin	– the Devil's Latin
Hin hales Latin	– Old Nick's Latin

The Paternoster itself is most probably a Christian replacement for an original pagan prayer or invocation.

Returning to *sueus* for a moment, the above interpretation might suggest that it served to provide magical sunshine inside the grave, an artificial and virtually eternal day which would prevent the deceased from rising to walk at night. With *sueus* shining, the night, for him, would not exist.

RUNEWORDS

Runewords are mostly found upon portable objects such as weapons or ornaments. Sometimes a translation can be made but not all runewords are linguistically translatable. As well as a full futhark, the Vadstena bracteate bears the word *luwatuwa*. The recurring group *uwa* suggests a possible sequence formula, which could offer interpretation by two statements: 'The strength of water is a pleasure to the God(s)' and 'The strength of victory is a pleasure to the God(s)', which could be applied to Njord, for instance.

The inscription of the owner's name on the Thames scramaseax would create a link between the use-potential of the weapon and the prowess of the owner. Such would also be the case with the sword in *Beowulf* which bore a gold plate engraved with the owner's name in runes. Adding a runic inscription to a tool or weapon would increase its usefulness immeasurably.

From Roman times onwards, weapons are known throughout the north marked with luck-bringing devices: swastika, boar (sacred to Frey and the Vanir), eye, cross and eventually runes. The Dahmsdorf spearhead bears a swastika and a triskele as well as *ranja* router. The Ovre Stabu spearhead bears *raunijaz*, 'tester' or 'prober'. These inscriptions mightily increase the weapons' effectiveness, giving their owners a vital psychological advantage. Words such as *latha* (invitation), *alu* (magic, taboo or protection) and *auja* (luck), appear on a variety of objects. A small, sixth century wooden sword from West Friesland, intended as a safe-conduct token, bears *edaboda*, meaning return-messenger.

The Darum bracteate from Jutland (c.450) bears *lathu* written backwards. *Lathu* means summons, and it is conceivable that its reversal might imply a banishing formula. There again, in all fairness, it could just have been the runemaster writing from right to left.

Sometimes runewords were inscribed in places where they wouldn't normally be seen and could work their magic in secret, unknown to any save the object's owner, and possibly even working on the same deliberate forgetfulness principle as some modern sigilization techniques. The Chessel Down sword chape bears the hidden inscription *aco sori*, increase pain, which the weapon was obviously intended to achieve.

FULL RUNIC INSCRIPTIONS

Full inscriptions aren't too common on portable objects, because of the restricted area available for inscribing, but are nonetheless found. A good example is the Strom whetstone, inscribed *wate hali hino horna haha skathi hathu ligi*, or 'Wet

Figure 10. The Chessel Down sword chape

78

this stone, horn. Scythe, scathe. Hay (or grain) lie.' This is obviously designed to add to the effectiveness of the whetstone in exactly the same way as an aggressive runeword adds to the efficiency of a weapon.

'Always carry this yew in the host of battle,' instructs the Britsum amulet, an overtly magical object. It must be said that full inscriptions frequently have little of the magical about them, pointing up the secular uses of runes as well as the more esoteric ones. Occasionally the two uses are combined, as with the Sigtuna copper box from the eleventh century. This bears a provenance for the merchant's precious-metal weighing scales it contains, and concludes with two lines of *drokkvaet*, considered the noblest skaldic metre, constituting a curse to keep thieves away.

The Ribe (human) skull fragment, which was pierced for wearing as an amulet, is overtly magical and dates from around 800, though it shows earlier letter-forms and thus supports the idea that the Common Germanic Futhark survived for cultic purposes. Its interpretation is difficult, but it has been identified as a charm invoking Odin (as psychopomp?) and others, giving protection against sickness.

Full inscriptions are often found on standing stones, many of which are memorials. Sometimes these may carry a curse to prevent the unscrupulous from destroying the stone or even carrying it away to erect elsewhere. The Björketorp stone bears a most unambiguous curse against such practices, promising a horrible death to anyone destroying it. Is it only a coincidence that it is still in place today?

Dedicating objects to a deity by means of an inscription also requires mention. The Thorsberg scabbard chape bears *Owlthuthewaz ni waje ma*, 'Servant of Ullr of immaculate repute'. This dedication is unusual in that the bow is the weapon most often associated with Ull.

RUNIC NUMEROLOGY

Many authors have tried to attribute some kind of numerological significance to the runes. Most of them have failed because they have either attempted to treat the runic alphabet in the same way as they might the Latin, Greek or Hebrew alphabets, attributing a specific numerical value to each rune, or they have not bothered to return to the source material from which a valid runic numerology may be derived.

The key to runic numerology lies in the way combinations and sequences of runes are assembled. While there is no reason to assume that individual runes have been employed to represent numbers, there is every reason for supposing that groups of the same rune vary in meaning according to the number of runes in the group.

REPEATED RUNES

It was long believed by the earliest Germanic runemasters that each rune was possessed of a spirit or power. One of the ways in which this power could be released was by concentrating this innate quality by repetition. Certainly the eddas provide evidence for the ascription of different meanings to different numbers, as will become apparent very shortly.

One

The monad of the ancients is perhaps the most difficult number to isolate from the evidence provided by the eddas. All items which aren't plural are singular, such as a tree, a weapon or a loaf. Single runes, as employed in the inscriptions and texts which have survived for study, often stand for their name-words and powers, unless modified by a sequence of troll-runes (which we shall examine later). In a sequence of individual runes, such as an aett or futhark, all the runes employed will be of equal power and value.

Two

Thor's chariot is drawn by two goats. When he travels into Jötunheim to meet Utgard-Loki, two children go with him as his servants. Hymir, fishing with Thor, catches two whales at a single cast. In *Hávamál*, Odin hangs his clothes upon two wooden stakes or effigies. In *Vafthrúdnismál*, two humans escape the Ragnarök. In *Grimnismál*, two horses draw the sun across the heavens. In *Lokasenna*, both Frey and Ægir have two servants. Two horses draw the moon. Odin has two wolves and two servants attending him. The sons of Bor create the first humans from two logs, an ash and an elm. There are two swans in Urd's well. In *Fjolsvinnsmál*, two fierce hounds stand sentinel. The goat Heidrun provides mead for all the heroes in Valhalla from her two teats. Freya's chariot is drawn by two cats.

From these examples it's possible to elicit that anything twofold in the eddas has some implication of servitude. Tyr is to be twice-named when engraving a sword with victory-runes, thus invoking his power and rendering it subservient to the will of the runemaster, that it might grant victory and aid to whomsoever might wield it.

Three

This is one of the more important numbers of practical runecraft. Yggdrasil has three roots which terminate at three wells. There are three chief Norns, Urd, Verdandi and Skuld, who control all human destiny. More than three measures of ale are drunk in *Thrymskvida*, the implication being that this amount is excessive. In *For Scirnis*, Skirnir scores three runes on a branch, on which he has previously cut a sequence of troll-runes, and uses it to threaten Gerd with thraldom to a three-headed troll. Three troll-runes are required to activate a troll-rune sequence. In *Völuspá*, Gullveig is thrice burned and thrice restored. The three gods who are the sons of Bor, namely Odin, Hoenir and Lodur, give life to the ash and elm logs which become the first humans. Thor owns three precious things: his iron gauntlets, his belt of strength and the hammer Mjölnir. Thor caught Loki at the third attempt when Loki was in his salmon-shape, and he was then bound by the gods to three rocks. Odin lies with Gunnlod for three nights in order to get close to the poetic mead Odraerir. She allows him three draughts of it. In the prophecy of the Ragnarök, three terrible winters, without other seasons intervening, will herald the final conflict. It took three days for the primeval cow, Audhumla, to lick Odin's ancestor Buri out of the ice. Snorri lists three kinds of dwarf and three kinds of Norn. Loki has three children by Angrboda: the Fenris Wolf, Hel, and the Midgard Serpent, Jörmungand. The Fenris Wolf is finally bound by the third fetter, Gleipnir. Whenever Hel Left Niflheim, she was supposed to have ridden a three-legged horse. In *Hávamál*, Loddfafnir is advised not to offer three words to one who is unworthy.

The number three has a further contribution to make to runecraft because of its link with the phases of the moon, and three is a number of great magical power. It is the root of nine, and there are nine worlds contained within Yggdrasil. Three kings taught or deluded Gylfi about the gods. The rainbow was said to have been formed from the blending of three colours, which accords well with the three primaries, red, yellow and blue, from which all the colours are derived. Groups of three runes appear on the Gummarp and Ellestad stones and many other surviving artefacts and monuments.

Four

Thor had to wade through four rivers in order to reach the lower-world Thingstead. Four harts gnaw the high branches of Yggdrasil and four serpents are named in the *Elder Edda* as hiding and gnawing beneath the tree. Four dwarves support the sky, made from the skull of Ymir, and Snorri has four rivers of milk flowing from the teats of Audhumla to feed the primeval frost-giant. At Baldur's funeral it took four berserkers to subdue the wolf-mount of the giantess Hyrokkin. Loki fled to a mountain-top and built himself a house with four doors so that he could see in every direction. In *Gylfaginning*, Gefjun uses four oxen to cheat the gods. The hero of *Gongu-Hrolf's Saga* is beset by magically-induced bad weather which is eventually traced to a group of sorcerers operating upon a platform supported by four columns. The dwarf Mondul carves counter-spells on these and the sorcerers perish horribly.

Thor's wading through the waters is a source of great inconvenience to him, as all the other gods simply had to ride across the rainbow-bridge Bifröst. The gnawing of the harts and serpents is obviously disadvantageous, to put it mildly, to Yggdrasil. Even the four dwarves can't be over-pleased at having to hold a giant's skull up for eternity, and the attempts of the berserkers to subdue Hyrokkin's wolf were not without discomfort. The number four thus yields an interpretation of, at the mildest, inconvenience, and, at the most extreme, severe annoyance, distress and discomfort.

Five

Five is mentioned by the author of the eddaic poem *Hárbardsljód*, where Odin/Harbard has spent five winters with Fjolver. The period was a cause of some satisfaction to him and proceeded well. Utgard-Loki derives great satisfaction from the failure of Thor and his companions to complete the five tests devised for them. Hymir's cauldron, stolen by Thor, is secreted five miles deep. In *Hávamál*, it is said that friendship flames hotter than fire in false friends for five days. Five is thus taken to denote general satisfaction and success.

Six

Six valkyries are named in *Völuspá*. As servants of Odin, they are opposed to his enemies. *Grimnismál* names six serpents which gnaw at Yggdrasil. The fetter Gleipnir uses to bind the Fenris Wolf is made from six magical materials. In *Vafthrúdnismál*, Ymir gives birth to a six-headed giant whose son is the proto-giant Bergelmir. On the sixth day friendship dies amongst false friends, according to *Hávamál*.

Gleipnir is unwelcome to the Fenris Wolf, which will be bound by it until the Ragnarök. False friends are similarly not welcomed. From this we may derive six as a number representing that which is either unwelcome or even a cause of downright hostility.

Seven

In *Hárbardsljód*, Odin dallies with seven sisters and has sexual relations with all of them. Volund and his brothers live happily with their swan-maiden brides for seven years. Seven can thus be taken as a number signifying sexual matters.

Eight

Thor's hall, Bilskirnir, has 640 (80 x 8) floors. Valhalla has 640 doors and 960 (80 x 12) warriors can emerge from each door at once. In *Grimnismál*, Odin doesn't move for eight nights. In *Thrymskvida*, Mjölnir is hidden eight miles deep and Loki claims that Thor, disguised as Freya, hasn't eaten for eight long nights. When he does he consumes, amongst other things, eight salmon. Eight servants and furnishings are

Figure 11. Odin on Sleipnir from the Alskog stone

noted in Hel's palace. Odin's grey mount, Sleipnir, has eight legs. In *Lokasenna* it is said that Loki lived under the earth for eight winters. (Note the continuing use of 'winter' as a unit of measure!) The three gods who made the first humans bestowed eight faculties and abilities upon them.

There are eight runes to an *aett* in the Common Germanic Futhark, and so eight is taken to be the number of a full set. It thus possesses the strength implied by such completeness. Eight is a trigger-number in the same way as three, but by increasing the length of the sequence, a corresponding increase in potency is achieved. The first sequence on the Lindholm amulet is one of eight A-runes, signifying God or Odin and representing a formidable invocation of that deity. This interpretation is reinforced by an inscription upon one of the other faces which reads *Ek erilaz sa wilagaz hateka* – 'I am of the Erilaz. I am called the cunning one.' The cunning one is one of the many titles of Odin.

Nine

Njord stayed only nine nights in the mountains beloved of his bride Skadi. The mothers of Heimdal are nine sisters. Hermod was nine nights riding down to Hel to speak with Baldur. During the Ragnarök, Thor kills Jörmungand, the Midgard Serpent, but survives only long enough to stagger back nine paces.

Overall nine appears to be the number of knowledge and completion. Eight and nine are linked in many places in the eddas. In *Hýmisqvida*, Thor breaks eight cauldrons whilst stealing the ninth. Draupnir drops eight new rings from itself every ninth night. Eight completes the period of waiting and nine brings fruition. In *Grimnismál*, Odin waits for the ninth night to reveal his true identity, having endured torture by fire on the eight preceding nights.

Thor kills Thrym on the ninth night and Gerd makes Frey wait nine nights for their wedding. (As we noted 'winter' as a measure, now we are also seeing 'night' in the same context!) In *Völuspá*, the sybil states that Yggdrasil links nine worlds and has nine roots. Odin hangs upon Yggdrasil for nine long nights to discover the runes. He learns nine lays of power and cites nine different medicines against the evils which beset mankind. Vafthrudnir is said to have wandered throughout nine worlds and nether-Hel. Nine maidens attend Menglad in *Svipdagsmál*. The same poem describes a magical sword protected by nine locks and Groa teaches her son nine charms to protect him on his travels.

Nine also appears in the sagas in a magical context similar to that of the protective magical circle of Judaeo-Christian tradition. In *Faereyinga Saga*, Thrand employed a necromantic process to try to learn the truth about Sigmund's death when he 'had great fires made up in the hall and four hurdles set to form a square. Then he marked out nine enclosures from the hurdles, in all directions, and sat upon a stool between the fires and the hurdles' and put himself into a trance.

In the ecclesiastical *Mariu Saga*, written sometime before 1238, a would-be seer is advised to go to a lonely forest and lay a freshly-flayed ox-hide on the ground. He should then draw nine squares about it, reciting 'devilish' incantations, then sit upon it until the devil comes to reveal the future. Even allowing for the way in which the Christian author has distorted the true nature of the rite, something of the flavour of old pagan northern sorcery survives in this account.

In *Gisli's Saga*, Bork pays the sorcerer Thorgrim Neb to work a vengeance spell for him. One of the ingredients, provided by Bork, is a nine-year-old ox. *Gisli's Saga* is mostly set in the period immediately after Iceland adopted Christianity, on 4 June 1000, and the crossover of cultures is readily apparent in much of its content.

Referring to an Anglo-Saxon charm, Gustav Storms illustrates a belief that nine spirits had taken up residence in a sore and required conjuring out before the sore would heal. This had to be done by means of an incantation which, by the arrangement of its text, diminished the number of spirits by one in each line until none remained in residence. This technique was popular in many medieval magical charms, where the written word had taken over from the spoken formula, with ABRACADABRA being a favourite candidate for this kind of diminution:

```
A B R A C A D A B R A
A B R A C A D A B R
A B R A C A D A B
A B R A C A D A
A B R A C A D
A B R A C A
A B R A C
A B R A
A B R
A B
A
```

However, it is important to remember that this was only possible once written literacy had been established, and that this kind of written charm would not have had a place in original northern magical practice.

From the evidence available, nine doesn't seem to have been used in magical rune-sequences. Eight would usually provide as complete, powerful and efficient a sequence as any runemaster could have required.

The Meanings of Runic Number Sequences

The meanings of runic number sequences can be summed up as follows.

One represents the name-word, or a meaning or power associated with the rune.

Two implies servitude or bondage.

Three is a trigger-number. A sequence of three troll-runes is required to activate the shape-shift or change of meaning in the runes which follow. Three is also the number of runes required for a lesser invocation.

Four signifies annoyance and discomfort.

Five brings general satisfaction and success, and as such is appropriate for healing purposes.

Six means inconvenience or that which is unwelcome.

Seven is linked to sexual matters.

Eight, like three, is a trigger-number. It signifies completion and strength and is the number of runes required for a greater invocation.

Nine may be taken to mean an even greater completion, with the eight taken as a whole which endorses and confirms it.

These meanings are qualified by the actual significance or interpretations placed upon the runes. There may, for example, be occasions when three troll-runes – ThThTh – merely imply a lesser invocation to the powers of the giants or trolls, and not the release of the shape-shift power. In the same way AAA may signify three gods, or DDDDD five days, as opposed to a lesser invocation of a deity or deities or a day of particular good fortune and success. The runemaster will learn to distinguish the most appropriate meaning of a sequence as his or her skill and aptitude increases.

TROLL-RUNES

One of the most important illustrations of a technique of runecraft is to be found in the eddaic poem describing how Scirnir won Gerd to be Frey's bride. The usual presents and blandishments had little effect upon the stubborn and reluctant Gerd, leading Scirnir to threaten the unfortunate maid with one of the longest and most terrible curses ever pronounced, though nowhere near as long as the Christian St Adelbert's curse against thieves. Eventually this curse produced the required reaction.

Having found a suitable branch for cutting the runes upon, Scirnir produces a curse which involves a remarkable collection of threats. These include possession by a three-headed troll and subsistence upon a diet of goat's-piss, all reinforced by the cuts he makes upon the branch:

> Troll-runes I cut, and then three more;
> Frenzy, filth and lust.
> Yet I'll scrape off each rune I grave
> If I find it has no need.

The interest this story has for us is not in the power of the curse so much as in the method Scirnir employs. The troll-rune is *Thurisaz*, and its use was thought to evoke demons from the nether-world. The three letters which follow, 'frenzy', 'filth' and 'lust', do not exist as such within any known futhark of the period. However, if troll-runes pervert or invert the meanings of those runes which follow it becomes possible that existing letters can have alternative meanings when preceded by such a sequence as a lesser invocation (three). *Wunjo* is usually taken to mean 'joy', but at least one source offers an interpretation of inducing madness, thus possibly identifying it as the 'frenzy' of Scirnir's curse. The meaning of *Pertho* is frequently disputed, with various meanings including dance, fruit-tree and hearth being put forward. The Anglo-Saxon runic poem offers chessman, but this is probably a late derivation. Leo, in *Runic and Heroic Poems*, compares it to the Slavonic word *pizda*, or vulva, and this reading, with fruit-tree, dance and hearth being taken as sexual euphemisms, would make *Pertho* the lust-rune for a woman and *Inguz* the lust-rune for a man in a troll-rune inscription. Filth is a little harder to identify, but as *Pertho* and *Wunjo* have been adapted by the preceding troll-runes it could be a modified meaning of *Kaunaz* in its interpretation of sore or abscess.

Scirnir scores the three troll-runes, then the three letters of the curse proper. This results in a total inscription of six characters, itself signifying inconvenience and a lack of welcome, both of which Gerd would have experienced! That a sequence of troll-runes is required to activate the change of meaning of succeeding runes is obvious for several reasons. To begin with, if only one *Thurisaz* was required then the futhark could not exist without the last twenty-one characters having a permanently altered meaning, and this was not the case. If it were, inscriptions such as those on the Strarup neck-ring, the Thorsberg chape and the Tune stone would not have been possible. The rune would have remained a potent but separate magical symbol, like the swastika and the triskele, and never have been employed for epigraphic purposes.

Two troll-runes would have brought the total number of runes in the inscription up to five, a number more applicable to Scirnir's enterprise than the effect he was attempting to create upon Gerd, the actual subject of the rune-spell. Three is far and away the most satisfactory number for the sequence, especially in view of three's role as a lesser invocation.

The alterations we may expect to the traditional meanings of the runes of the Common Germanic Futhark, as a result of their taking a place in a troll-rune sequence, are as follows:

FEHU	– poverty	EIWAZ	– loss of skill
URUZ	– loss of strength	PERTHO	– female lust
THURISAZ		ALGIZ	– defencelessness
ANSUZ	– cursing	SOWULO	– scorching heat
RAIDO	– storms	TEIWAZ	– defeat
KENAZ	– filth	BERKANA	– sterility
GEBO	– meanness	EHWAZ	– uncertainty
WUNJO	– frenzy	MANNAZ	– adversity
HAGALAZ	– floods	LAGUZ	– drought
NAUTHIZ	– disablement	INGUZ	– male lust
ISA	– treachery	OTHILA	– loss of inheritance
JERA	– famine, shortage	DAGUZ	– darkness

Figure 12. The meanings of troll-runes

THE NUMBER OF RUNES IN A SEQUENCE

A new aspect of magical rune-use has now emerged, in that while the number of times a particular rune is repeated has a meaning of its own, it must also relate to the overall number of runes making up the sequence.

Thus *Gebo* following three troll-runes will promote meanness. Three troll-runes and *Fehu* will mean poverty. Three troll-runes and *Uruz* signify weakness. Each of these sequences totals four runes in all, appropriate in view of that number's significance.

The same is also true of sequences which do not contain troll-runes. The word on the Dahmsdorf spearhead, *ranja*, translated as router, has five letters as well as a meaning. Five would offer its owner satisfaction and success, the very attributes he would require when wielding the weapon. The

Kowell spearhead has *tilarids*, both a word meaning 'goal-seeker' and a sequence of eight.

In cases where the number of runes in a word or sequence might not be appropriate to its meaning there were at least two techniques available to the runemaster. One was the use of *bindrunar* or ligatures to bring the total number of characters to an acceptable and appropriate figure. The second was the addition of a magical symbol or symbols, such as the triskele or swastika.

H.R. Ellis Davidson puts up an acceptable case for identifying the swastika with Thor's hammer, while admitting the swastika to be the older of the two signs. The identification can be reinforced from other sources, and it is abundantly clear that such signs, together with the lightning flash also attributed to Thor, while not themselves runes, may be considered to have a value much greater than that of simple decoration. This technique was known to, among others, the inscriber of the Værløse clasp, who added a swastika to a rune sequence of six, making up the word *alugod* or 'magic good', to bring it up to a more acceptable seven symbols.

There will always be exceptions to these rules, as there will

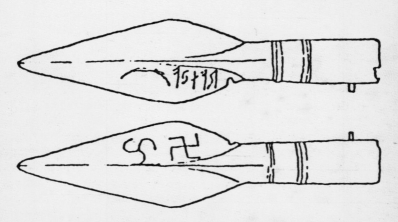

Figure 13. The Dahmsdorf spearhead

91

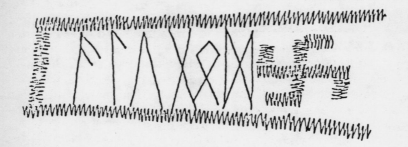

Figure 14. The Værløse Clasp

be to the numerology itself. While the runemaster responsible for the Værløse clasp knew what he was doing numerologically it should not be assumed that every runemaster did. Here is a valid overlap with modern magical practices. If the runes work for you it doesn't matter in the slightest if you're breaking the rules. But the trick is to know which of the rules you may break with impunity, and that means knowing them all in the first place.

6 · USING THE RUNES FOR DIVINATION

The best-known use of runes is divinatory, and it would be both inaccurate and unfair to pretend that this did not form a major part of the runemaster's stock-in-trade. The way in which runes were both used and prepared goes back as far as the known use of the symbols, with the *Germania* of Tacitus setting the basic principles which have been followed ever since.

The phrase 'casting the runes' has had an unwarranted and emotive connotation ever since it was used by M.R. James as the title of a short story. The tale, filmed with the obligatory American hero as *Night of the Demon*, describes the attempts of a sorcerer, allegedly based on Aleister Crowley, to avenge a slight. The practice involved in the story is a form of cursing which bears very little resemblance to any runic practice. Firstly, the sorcerer's runes are written, not cut. Secondly, there is nothing in the text to prompt an assumption that the runes were connected to the sorcerer Karswell by the use of his blood. The story is simply fiction, albeit a superior chiller, and as such need not concern us.

In actuality casting the runes refers to the method by which they are precipitated, or cast, on to a white cloth for divinatory purposes, as described by Tacitus in AD 98. It will be beneficial to examine this account phrase by phrase.

THE OLDEST ACCOUNT OF RUNIC DIVINATION

Tacitus was writing around the time of the earliest extant runic finds. He states that the northern peoples had the highest regard for omens and the casting of lots, always following the same procedure. A branch was cut from a tree (Mattingley has nut-bearing, other translators have fruit-bearing, which widens the scope quite substantially – a nut may be a fruit but not vice-versa) and cut up into strips (small pieces). These pieces were marked with different characters, which have been reliably identified as runes, and then cast at random on to a white cloth.

The next stage depended upon whether the reading was for the tribe, an individual or a family unit. For the tribe, or state, a priest would have picked up three strips, one at a time, and interpreted them according to the signs marked thereon, having offered a prayer to the gods and looked skywards to avert his eyes while making the selection. For the family or an individual, it was the 'father', according to Tacitus, who would have made the selection. 'Father' is the usual translation, despite the statement less than 200 words away that there resides a special gift of holiness and prophecy in woman.

The sex of the runecaster remains ambiguous. 'Father' can easily be a mistranslation, or even sexist Roman interpretation, of a phrase meaning 'head of the family'. It has to be conceded that the Romans, descended as they were from a she-wolf, would not have taken a matriarchy at face value but imposed their own values. The runecaster could as easily have been female as male.

Yet here we have the basics, and these are basics which can be expanded upon to recreate the original practice of runic divination.

MAKING YOUR OWN RUNES

To begin at the beginning, anyone who has purchased a set of runes might just as well throw them out of the window right now. The only set worth possessing is that which you have made yourself, from the wood of a fruit-bearing tree.

Choosing a tree is mostly down to inclination. The majority of trees bear fruit of one kind or another, even if that fruit is inedible to humans. Beech bears beech-nuts. Yew bears berries, and if you spit the pips out the bulk of the berry isn't poisonous. Ash bears keys for the propagation of its species. Oak bears acorns, which pigs can eat even if humans don't relish them, though they have been used to make an ersatz coffee.

Some trees are obviously more favoured than others, but the choice remains personal. Ash is a strongly runic tree by implication, the world-ash Yggdrasil being the tree from which Odin hung in order to obtain the runes. Yew and birch are trees which have been specifically mentioned as runes, and as such have to be preferred woods. Apples from the Goddess Idun's casket kept the Norse gods young, and the apple is an obvious fruit-bearing tree, even if the northern wild species fruited with small, sour apples that today we wouldn't bother with, except perhaps for crab-apple jelly.

Before you go any further it is as well to decide which futhark or futhork you wish to work with. Here we are concentrating on the Common Germanic Futhark, but you may wish to work with the later Viking or Anglo-Saxon versions. Possibly you may want to experiment with all three, in which case it is as well to make three separate sets of runes rather than do a 'mix'n'match' with the common letters. This would mean you had to sort your runes out before you started, obtruding meanings into your consciousness which might not accord with the casting once made. Which set you work with will also determine how much wood you will need.

Select your tree, then, making sure you have permission from the owner, take the branch from which you intend to cut your runes. This need for permission is to ensure no unwelcome influences later manifest to corrupt the use of your runes. The Northern Mysteries contain a strong element of respect for nature and the environment, so try to take the wood in such a way that minimal damage is caused to the tree. You may feel the need to make it some kind of thank-offering.

There's no insistence in the Northern Mysteries, as there is in some branches of Wicca, that the work of taking the wood be done within a circle with a white-handled knife. The best tools are a saw for cutting the branch, a plane or sander for creating a flat surface, and a craft scalpel for actually cutting the fine detail of the letter-forms. These tools do not need to be 'virgin' or even specifically dedicated to their purpose, but virginity of intent throughout the operation of creating your runes should be a consideration. Use the sharpest tools you can, for two reasons. The first is that the wood will work more willingly with sharp tools. The second, in the event of an accident, is that blunt tools cause jagged cuts that may take longer to heal.

If you are cutting a branch, make the first cut to a depth of at least a quarter of an inch all the way around the branch in a complete circle before you begin to saw all the way through. This will prevent the bark tearing with the weight of the falling wood and thus avoid unnecessary damage.

With the wood selected and prepared it's time to cut the runes. You may wish to wait for a special day, such as a Wednesday in honour of Odin, or phase of the moon, such as nearly full. Pencil the shapes on lightly so that you'll know where and what to cut. Practise on a spare piece before you begin, feeling the qualities of the wood through the knife or scalpel you're using. Make shallow cuts to begin with. You can always widen them later but a piece once cut away cannot be replaced. If you're worried about a cut overshooting tape the piece of wood down firmly and hold a metal ruler at the bottom of the cut to check the blade.

Next you'll need something to keep them in. A leather or skin bag tied with a thong works as well as anything, though for a special set you may decide to take extra wood from the tree and slice it up to make a box of the same wood as the runes it is to contain. In either case, you need a container of some kind from which the runes can be cast, if they are too large for you to hold all twenty-four in the cupped palms of your hands. You will also need a white cloth which is simply something to cast them on to wherever you find yourself. It serves to keep them clean and avoid contamination from any influences which may be held in the piece of furniture or ground on to which they would otherwise fall.

With your runes created, you are close to beginning the process of divination. However, before we come to suggested meanings for the runes in a divinatory context, we must know how to complete the reading.

CASTING THE RUNES

According to Tacitus, the rune-caster, holding the runes ready to cast them on to the cloth, looks skywards and offers a prayer to the gods. The prayer is, in fact, an invocation, and the most appropriate deity to invoke is Odin, master of wisdom and winner of the runes for mankind. Bearing this in mind, the most appropriate invocation would be the first two verses of the *Runatál* from Chapter 3:

> I know I hung on the wind-swept tree,
> Its roots to the wise unknown;
> Spear-pierced, for nine long nights,
> To Odin pledged, self offered to self,
>
> They gave no bread, nor drinking horn;
> Down into the depths I gazed:
> Crying aloud I took up runes,
> Then finally I fell.

casting the runes as you reach the words 'Then finally I fell'.

The number of runes to be selected for the reading ultimately depends upon personal preference, as do the interpretations you place on the symbols. Tacitus says that three of the runes are picked up and interpreted. Bearing in mind that the most important numbers in northern magic are three, eight and nine, this is a good starting number. In order to obtain a more detailed reading I suggest that, as you become more confident, you take two further groups of three, giving you nine runes in total. This combines both three and nine, following the 'feel' of the system.

With experience, you may well come to devise a method of your own. Freya Aswynn works with twelve runes, linking them to the astrological houses. I eschew both the tarot and astrology as southern interpolations and work with the three groups of three. I take a casting as complete if the rune *Ehwaz* should appear, as Tacitus continues to describe a method of deriving omens from horses which suggests an attribution of confirmation as one of the meanings of this rune. Both techniques are equally valid, and it cannot be stressed too strongly or too often that the runes lend themselves to personal application and interpretation better than any other form of psychic tool.

WHEN TO CAST THE RUNES

With the technique described, the only further consideration, apart from the meanings, is the time selected for the casting. The means of determining this can be as simple or complex as you like. Again, it is individual trial and error that will reveal what is best for you. There is no reason to suppose that the hours of darkness are better than the hours of daylight, or vice versa. Nor is any day of the week to be thought better than any other. However, Nigel Pennick, in *Practical Magic in the Northern Tradition*, ascribes a rune to each hour, and you may wish to make your casting in a runic hour appropriate to the question being asked. This is described in more detail in Chapter 7.

Another alternative, somewhat more limiting, can be taken from Tacitus, who had a great sympathy for the northern tribes he was writing about. The tribes that used the runes had a great regard for the moon, and considered the most auspicious times for embarking on any enterprise as shortly after the new moon or immediately before the full moon. The phases of the moon play an important part in northern magic and are related to the Nornir, or Fates, of Norse mythology. This might incline you to believe that castings during the waxing moon are more reliable than those made when it is on the wane, and that the worst time would be during the dark of the moon, known to the northern people as the 'glimpses of the moon', and a time when ghosts and demons walked abroad and created evil in the world of men. Ghosts especially, rather than the Christian concept of demons, were physical manifestations to be feared, and it was often necessary for the Icelandic exorcist to wrestle them back into their graves.

As a final thought on timing, again relating to the Norns and the phases of the moon, the following is offered:

Urd	First quarter	Past
Verdandi	Full moon	Present
Skuld	Last quarter	Future

This enables you to relate the question to the time, linking with both the moon and the Norns and invoking the added benefit of their influence. For instance, 'Would it have been better if Ingrid had done so-and-so?' is an Urd/First quarter question, relating to the past. 'Is Ingrid doing so-and-so?' is a Verdandi/Full moon question, relating to the present. And 'Will Ingrid do so-and-so?' is a Skuld/Last quarter question, requiring an answer regarding a future action.

INTERPRETING YOUR CASTING

The question of interpretation now arises. Once more this is ultimately individual, with decisions to be made. No decision need ever be final, though, and the wise runecaster will be constantly modifying and improving his or her personal system in the light of experience. What works for you works for YOU.

The basic questions to be answered before you begin to interpret a casting are as follows.

1. Do I have a full set of interpretations for the futhark/futhork I am going to work with?

2. Do I wish to make any personal alterations to the meanings which have been given, or impose extra interpretations upon them?

3. Do I wish to regard upside-down runes as having a negative (or other) influence upon the meaning?

The first question will have been dealt with before you made your runes and need only detain you if you begin to feel that you would be better off working with another futhark/futhork. The second question is one that can only be answered with time and experience. A suggested list of meanings for the Common Germanic Futhark is given below as an interim measure. Those for other sets can be derived from the respective rune poems. Still the best version of the rune poems is *Runic and Heroic Poems* by Bruce Dickins.

The third question is the most complex of the three. If we look at the shapes of the runes we see that some will look the same upside-down, preventing an alternative meaning. Interestingly enough there are nine of these. You may feel that the remaining fifteen will give you added diversity and room to think your way around the casting. Or you might be a purist and feel that inverted runes are too close to upside-down tarot cards, and remembering that the tarot was never native to the northern lands prefer to eschew inversion. The best answer is the one you feel to be right for you, remembering that it can always be modified if experience should prove it to be incorrect on a personal basis.

THE MEANINGS OF THE RUNES

Suggested meanings for the runes as used in divination are listed here only as an interim measure. Eventually your own meanings and methods of interpretation will come to you. No account is taken of inversion, but as a general rule, if you decide to use inverted runes, the meaning will be the opposite of the one given.

FEHU   Financial strength and prosperity in the present or near future. Possessions won or earned.

URUZ Physical strength and speed. This can relate either to the enquirer or to others.

THURISAZ   Conflicts and complexities of an aggressive nature. Unreliability. A tendency towards change.

ANSUZ   Blessings, especially connected with religion. The consolation of faith.

R RAIDO   Travel, both in physical terms and those of life-style direction. The right move for you to make and deciding upon it.

< KAUNAZ   The possibility of adverse health and general mental or physical malaise or unpleasantness.

X GEBO   Gifts, in both the senses of sacrifice and generosity. All matters relating to exchanges, including contracts and personal relationships.

P WUNJO   Joy, pleasure, but also the possibility of going 'over the top'. If restrained, the meaning is general success and recognition of worth.

H HAGALAZ   Uncontrolled forces, either within in the unconscious or without in the physical world, especially weather.

+ NAUTHIZ   Restriction caused by need. Hard work ultimately bringing relief from suffering due to financial constraints.

I ISA   Psychological blocks to thought or activity, including grievances. In a casting this rune reinforces the meanings of those around it.

< JERA   Hopes and expectations of peace and prosperity. The promise of success. The results of earlier efforts are realized.

ʃ EIHWAZ   The driving force to acquire, providing motivation and a sense of purpose.

< PERTHO   Female concerns and mysteries, including female fertility. Creativity waiting to come to fruition.

Y ALGIZ   The protective urge to shelter oneself or others. Keeping hold of success or maintaining a position won or earned.

SOWULO The life-force. Good health or other favourable circumstances and future harmony. Contact between the higher self and the unconscious.

TEIWAZ Knowing where your true strengths lie. General success and success in legal matters. Honour, justice, leadership and authority.

BERKANA General fertility, both mental and physical, and personal growth. The prospering of an enterprise or venture.

EHWAZ Status as it relates to oneself and others. A message from the Gods. In a casting this rune confirms beyond doubt the meanings of those runes around it.

MANNAZ The individual or race. Your attitude towards others and their attitudes towards you. Friends and enemies.

LAGUZ Success in travel or acquisition, but with the possibility of loss. Imagination and psychic matters.

INGUZ Male fertility and expectations on a physical level, including matters of health, family and progeny.

OTHILA Inheritance. Your home, including physical patrimony, spiritual heritage, experience and fundamental values.

DAGAZ Security and certainty. Daylight clarity as opposed to night-time uncertainty. A time to plan or embark upon an enterprise.

There are differing opinions regarding any role the *ættir* might have in a casting. Freya Aswynn orders her meanings so that the first *ætt* deals with things on the most basic level and concerns itself with the outer world. The second goes much deeper into the psychological make-up of the individual, concerning itself with inner considerations. The third *ætt* transcends the first two, concentrating on relationships with others and seeking to provide a synthesis and integration of the first two.

My personal preference is to keep later psychological disciplines away from any magical procedure and strip it back to basics, in so far as modern man with the various influences imposed upon him is capable of doing. Again, this is an area for personal preference to dictate.

With the above information you are ready to begin your first experiments in runic divination. Like all psychic techniques it may not come quickly, but it will eventually. Persistence works wonders.

7 · WORKING WITH THE RUNES

However you decide to work with the runes, whether for healing, self-improvement, divination or in any area of northern magical practice, for real success you need to make them a part of your daily life. There are a variety of ways of doing this. The simplest is to make or buy a ring or pendant which has the runes engraved upon it. There are several on the market ready-made, if you look around, but the best are those personal ones which you either make yourself, if you have the skill, or have made for you. If you can cut your own set of runes with a craft scalpel, then you can cut a full futhark on a smaller scale on a piece of the same wood trimmed, holed, thonged and hung about your neck. Yew is an ideal wood for this because of its strength, even in quite thin sections. This chapter suggests how and when runes can be integrated into daily life.

THE RUNIC CLOCK

In *Practical Magic in the Northern Tradition* Nigel Pennick describes a runic clock, attributing one of each of the twenty-four hours of the day to one of the twenty-four runes of the Common Germanic Futhark. He describes the time period of an hour as beginning as half-past the hour before and continuing until half-past the hour itself. For example, the rune *Jera* covers midnight, with the hour running from 11.30 pm to 12.30 am (23.30 to 00.30 on the twenty-four hour clock). The other runes follow in sequence according to the order of the futhark, and the day begins with *Fehu*, which runs from 12.30 pm to 1.30 pm (12.30 to 13.30).

This is one way of constructing a runic clock. However, if you take the old northern belief that the day began at sunset the day before, you might wish to start the day with *Fehu* at, say, 6.00 pm (18.00) as an average sunset time. The old pagan idea of night ushering in day is why so many 'eve' festivals still survive today. May Eve is the legendary *Walpurgisnacht*, when witches ride to the sabbat and all (non-Christian) evil is abroad. A famous eve still surviving, even revived to the disquiet of the fundamentalists in modern times, is Hallowe'en, the Eve of All Saints, upon which the friendly dead return to visit those left behind and unfriendly children threaten us with American 'trick or treat' demands.

You might wish to take the purist attitude of the medieval magician and actually discover what time sunset is and base the beginning of your day on that actual time, altering the times of the hours for each day. Alternatively that might feel unnecessarily complex, and you may wish to adopt the simplest runic clock, with *Fehu*'s hour starting at midnight (00.00) and continuing until 1.00 am (01.00).

Whatever you decide, and because work with the runes is so personal, this is a decision you can make for yourself, even if you later discover it to be inadequate and elect to revise it. The purpose of the runic clock is to become aware of the feel of each rune at the appropriate hour of the day. Obviously if you are to complete this successfully you'll need an alarm clock and a flexible schedule at some point, but the exercise is worth pursuing for the extra personal understanding of both runic meanings and runic attributions it will impart.

RUNES AND THE CALENDAR

With sufficient mathematical skill one can fit any sequence of numbers to any other sequence of numbers. Nigel Pennick

105

relates the twenty-four runes to one twenty-fourth of the year, a period equivalent to fifteen days, five hours and various minutes and seconds, making half of an averaged month and closely allied to a fortnight. A simpler method of doing this is to take your calendar and, on the middle and last day of each month, change to the next rune in the sequence. This may not be so accurate, but it will give you the flavour of the runes as they run through the year.

Remember that this is personal to you, so experiment as to which runes you set when. For example, you might want to place *Jera*, the harvest rune, in the last half of August or the first half of September. See which feels right as the year progresses. As February is usually the coldest month, try setting *Isa* there and feel how it works for you. The fact that *Jera* follows might just as easily relate to the nascent Spring and the burgeoning new life 'springing' from the earth.

There are eight festivals in the pagan year which are listed in more detail later in this chapter. Eight has already been noted as one of the more potent numbers of runecraft. Try setting three runes to each festival and see how it influences your appreciation of them. Later, when we come to a specimen devotional framework, an example of this will be provided.

THE DAYS OF THE WEEK

One Christian feast which has become an inescapable and regular part of everyone's life is Sunday. Based on the same idea, though on a different day, as the Jewish (Old Testament) sabbath, Sunday is an official day of rest riddled with paradox and perplexity. Sunday trading laws in England are a shambles. Officially you can buy soft porn but not a copy of the Bible. Six days a week (with the exception of Good Friday) you can buy wine for a private devotion at 4.00 o'clock in the afternoon, but on Sunday it's illegal. Sunday is the day of no work, unless you count cooking the Sunday lunch, washing the car, catching up on jobs around the house, amusing the children, cutting the lawn ... It is the day upon which the Lord is said to have rested, so everyone else is supposed to do so as well, whether they want to or not. This is being written on a Sunday! It is also the one day of the week on which some couch Christians make an effort to worship.

Christianity 'legitimized' the major pagan feasts. By instituting Sunday for worship it also took over an individual feast day which pagans reserved for a particular deity. The days of the week all bore names which referred to deities of one form or another. For example, our Wednesday in Old Norse was *Odinsdagr*, in Dutch *Woensdag*, in Anglo-Saxon *Wodenesdaeg* and in Swedish and Danish *Onsdag*. Friday was *Friadagr* in Old Norse, *Vrijdag* in Dutch and *Frigedaeg* in Anglo-Saxon. Tuesday and Thursday can also be clearly traced back to their deity roots. Saturday may safely be assumed for Loki, though the etymology is admittedly tortuous and confirmed more by custom than scholarship. The days of the week were attributed as follows:

Sunday	The sun
Monday	The moon
Tuesday	Tyr
Wednesday	Odin
Thursday	Thor
Friday	Freya
Saturday	Loki

This scheme is basically Roman in its origination and relies upon the Romanization of Norse deities for its verification. The sun and moon were never regarded as major deities in the north, but it is worth noting that their gender was not the same as further south, with the sun being feminine and the moon masculine. This would make Sunday, assuming the attribution to the sun is still held, a goddess day, to the despair of Christians everywhere. Yet there is also the consideration of Baldur as a solar deity to take into account. Sunday and Monday are free under the above scheme to be attributed to deities of your choice. One suggestion would be to take Sunday as a day of the goddess, without the need to refer it to the sun. Monday is open to many interpretations. The Nornir can be said to represent the moon's phases. It could also be attributed to Hel as an underworld deity, whence the moon emerges and returns to, or any other deity the individual worshipper feels appropriate. In short, you can assign deities to either day in whichever way feels most comfortable to you.

MONTHS

Several attempts have been made to identify the months with the signs of the zodiac, but these are doomed to failure for a variety of reasons. To begin with, our forefathers were too far north to be able to see all twelve signs. Zodiac lore originated in the Middle East, and while it moved north with the passage of time it had little relevance in Scandinavia.

While there was star-wisdom in the north, there is no evidence to show that it bore any connection with the zodiac. In the early days, when the lunar year of thirteen months held sway, each month was computed from one new moon to the next, and the zodiac would not have held any significance, even if it had been known. In later times, with the solar calendar replacing the old lunar one, individual months became more significant. Both Norse and Anglo-Saxon lists of months are available. The names frequently referred to the characteristic weather which was to be expected, or to the time of year or to a festival contained within the period.

One intriguing idea which is worth examining is that the twelve homes of the Gods referred to in *Grimnismál* are related to the twelve months of the year:

1.	Thor	Thrúdheim [land of strength]
2.	Ull	Ydalir [yew-dale]
3.	Frey	Alfheim [elf-home]
4.	Frigg	Sökkvabekkr [sunken-bench]
5.	Odin	Gladsheim [glad-land]
6.	Skadi	Thrymheim [sound-land]
7.	Baldur	Breidablik [broad-shining]
8.	Heimdal	Himinbjörg [heaven's-mount]
9.	Freya	Folkvangr [folk-field]
10.	Forseti	Glitnir [glistening]
11.	Njord	Noatún [harbour]
12.	Vidar	Vidi [wooden]

Several of these names are evocative of weather conditions.

Glitnir has a distinctly frosty feel to it. *Sökkvabekkr* reminds us of the dampness of February Fill-dyke, while *Breidablik* and *Himinbjörg* conjure a sun which is bright, strong and high in the heavens. The verses in *Grimnismál* contain much more information, plus a little confusion, and are well worth examining. The same is true, though over a greater range of topics, for almost every poem in the *Elder Edda*.

DIRECTIONS AND TIME

For any human there are four directions – before, behind, right and left, and together with observations of the sun's (apparent) motion these soon became translated almost universally into directions to help man around the surface of his planet. Northern peoples typically took their 'orientation' (eastwardness) from the north, remembering that we are now at least upon the fringes of the Land of the Midnight Sun. Observed north and south mark the winter and summer solstices. Perceived east and west are confirmed by the vernal and autumnal equinoxes. Thus four quarters of the horizon may be perceived to exist. In Norse myth they were supported by four dwarves called Nordri, Sudri, Austri and Vestri, who were set there when the sons of Bor (who was Odin's father) made the world from the flesh and bones of the giant Ymir.

Yet a more accurate designation of time than the four basic directions could provide was required by the daily lives of our forefathers. It was thus that the four quarters were further sub-divided to produce a total of eight directions, each one equivalent to a time of day. And with this designation, still observed in Iceland less than a century ago among families without a clock, other attributions came to be associated.

Midnight naturally related to the north, the darkest quarter. With this established, the other attributions followed readily. North-east represented the small hours of the morning, that time between midnight and dawn when the human spirit is at its lowest, usually refreshing itself in sleep. The east obviously corresponded to sunrise from observed phenomena, and the south to mid-day, which has always been taken in the north as the time when the sun was due south. The period in between, represented by the south-east, was the morning itself, with the earth warming and man warming to his labours. As the sun began to decline after noontide, so the day began to decline as well, making the south-west the period of afternoon. Sunset, in the west, brought the beginning of night, and the north-west represented that period of day which was between the twilight and the blackness of midnight.

THE PHASES OF THE MOON

When we examined runic divination, we related, in passing, the phases of the moon to the three *ættir* of the Common Germanic Futhark. Yet at the risk of introducing an anomaly, the actual phases of the moon might be considered as four, not three: first quarter, full, last quarter and *dark*.

The runes are logical enough to provide order, but also illogical enough to present contradictions. Three phases of the moon fit well with three *ættir* of the futhark. Four phases require a division of the twenty-four runes into four groups of six. Yet if this works for you, it is also right for you. It cannot be said too often that the runes represent a personal system, despite the dogmatism of some other authors, and that personal experimentation will best provide the way in which you interact with them most efficiently.

PERSONAL DEVOTION

From the above information we may begin to derive some concept of how the days, months and years of our northern forebears were constructed. With this in mind we are able to begin to work out a framework upon which both actions and devotions may be based.

For the runes to serve you as fully as they can, you will need to be in tune with the traditions and mythology behind them. A personal identification with a Norse deity is a highly efficient means of achieving this attunement. One of the objects of any devotional ritual is a very close identification with one's deity.

Even Christianity acknowledged this through St Thomas à Kempis' *The Imitation of Christ*.

One can relate to the gods in two ways. The first is by identification, which is easiest if the deity is of the same gender as yourself but far from impossible if the deity is of the opposite gender. The second way is by polarizing with the deity, in other words identifying with his or her consort. For instance, if a woman should worship Thor she might identify with Sif, unless she were a very strong female in which case a straight identification with Thor would be possible. However, there can be a heavy price to pay if that is the case, in terms of possibly taking on more attributes of the opposite sex than she might wish to aspire to.

To make identification easier, either with the deity or its consort, examine its character and physical attributes. Are there any physical correspondences between you and your chosen deity? (Yes, my right hand isn't as strong as the left so I have a possible link to Tyr.) Next look at the character of the god or goddess. How do they behave in a certain mythical situation? What would you do in this situation? Would you react more or less in the same manner, according to the same set of circumstances? Are there any other correspondences, such as likes or dislikes? For example, a love of jewellery, especially necklaces, would correspond with attributes of the Goddess Freya. This identification will happen, more or less, as a natural process.

Devotion is more than simply worshipping one's deity. Worship implies distance in terms of high and low, deity and supplicant. Unless some attempt is made to incorporate the characteristics and attributes of the deity concerned, which is the true means by which a deity can be realized on our plane of existence, no actual manifestation will genuinely occur. The idea of the technique involved is that we infuse ourselves with the energy of our god. We become that god and then, when we have entered the assumed identity of that deity, we can actually exert some portion of the deity's power. For example, you can perform a magical act of intent or offer a statement of intent with a greater chance of success than if you attempt a similar action as an ordinary human being.

It should be observed that traditional witchcraft follows the same eightfold festival pattern postulated below and related to the Norse concepts of direction and time. That the feasts were important dates across the cultures is evidenced by the way in which they have been Christianized and still survive today:

Yule = Norse Mother-Night = Christmas
February Eve (Feb 2nd) = Celtic Imbolc = Candlemas/
Purification of the Blessed Virgin Mary
Spring Equinox (Mar 21st) = Norse/Celtic Ostara
= Feast of St Benedict
(Mar 25 = Annunciation of the Blessed Virgin Mary)
May Eve = Norse Valburg = Celtic Beltane =
Feast of St Catherine of Siena
(May Day = Feasts of SS Philip and James [apostles])
Summer Solstice (Jun 21st) = Norse/Celtic Midsummer =
Feast of St Aloysius Gonzaga
(Jun 24th = Birthday [!] of St John Baptist)
August Eve = Celtic Lammas = Feast of
St Ignatius of Loyola
Autumn Equinox (Sep 21st) = Celtic Mabon =
Feast of St Matthew (apostle)
Hallowe'en = Norse beginning of winter =
Celtic Samhain = Vigil of All Saints,
preceding the Feast of All Saints on Nov 1st

It might be argued that the Church has a saint's day virtually every day of the year, and certainly it does. But these special dates were taken over by the Church in exactly the same way that pagan sites were. True, some of the feasts listed are comparatively late institutions, but a little research will show they have replaced earlier and less reputable Catholic luminaries for the most part.

A DEVOTIONAL FRAMEWORK

The deities in the scheme outlined in Figure 15 are based on my personal preferences and, like all the examples which have been provided, should serve only as a guide. It has deliberately been left incomplete. Explore and then use your own preferred correspondences, rather than those provided by someone else, for the best personal results. This is simply a skeletal outline which you can employ to begin building that devotional schema which you feel to be most appropriate for you. Some correspondences have been included. These would be used in building up ritual details, observing synchronicities and generally enriching your personal runic system. Again, nothing is fixed and the system which will work best for you is the one you devise.

The content and layout of each column is reasonably self-explanatory. Column 1 contains the rune-names according to the Common Germanic Futhark, but laid out in an order which may be unfamiliar. It is based upon the runic wheel in Freya Aswynn's book *Leaves of Yggdrasil*, and begins in the northern ætt of that wheel with *Isa*, *Jera* and *Eihwaz*. It then continues clockwise with the final grouping of *Wunjo*, *Hagalaz* and *Nauthiz* to north-west. The others contain the direction and phase of the moon attributed, and would refer to devotions throughout a lunar month and the direction to which they might be addressed, a time of day appropriate to each of the eight directions, together with a seasonal pagan festival and a colour. The festivals follow both the directions and their timing throughout the year in order. The colours progress logically according to their attributed stations and appropriateness for the seasonal festivals.

There is also a general time of day according to the clock as it appears, without benefit of BST, at either equinox, a deity attributed to the time and the direction and an elemental attribution. The elemental attributions would alter for some people if ice is taken as a fifth northern element, in that earth would then take a central place within, as opposed to around, the circle, and ice would replace earth where it is mentioned in this column.

Having now established a framework within which devotions may be assigned, the question arises as to how they should be performed. The eight major festivals are best shared in some way, either with close friends or fellow worshippers. The same is true for any celebrations of the lunar month you

THE ELEMENTS OF THE RUNES

DEVOTIONAL FRAMEWORK 1

Rune	Meaning	Power	Weapon	Animal	Bird	Tree	Deity	Time	Colour
ISA	Ice	Reinforce	Skis/Sled	Reindeer		Alder	SKADI	23.00	
JERA	Year	Plenty	Scythe				SIF	00.00	Black
EIWAZ	Yew	Hunt	Bow			Yew	ULL	01.00	
PERTHO	Vagina	F/fertile	Distaff	Woman	Heron	Elm	FRIGG	02.00	
ALGIZ	Defence	Protect	Blowhorn	Elk		Lime	HEIMDAL	03.00	Green
SOWULO	Sun	Lifeforce	Shield		Eagle	Oak	BALDUR	04.00	
TEIWAZ	Victory	Legal win	Sword			Hazel	TYR	05.00	
BERKANA	Growth	Enterprise		Bear	Swan	Birch	URD	06.00	Yellow
EHWAZ	Horse	Confirm	Box	Horse		Apple	IDUN	07.00	
MANNAZ	Man	Species		Man	Hawk			08.00	
LAGUZ	Water	Source	Axe	Seal	Gull	Willow	NJORD	09.00	Orange
INGUZ	Penis	M/fertile	Helmet	Boar	Cuckoo		FREY	10.00	
OTHILA	Inherit	Estate	Seat			Hawthorn	VALI	11.00	
DAGAZ	Day	Security				Rowan	VERDANDI	12.00	Red
FEHU	Cattle	Wealth	Necklace	Cat	Swallow	Elder	FREYA	13.00	
URUZ	Aurochs	Achieve	Shoe	Aurochs			VIDAR	14.00	
THURISAZ	Giant	Malchange	Knife	Snake		Blackthorn	LOKI	15.00	Purple
ANSUZ	God	Blessing	Spear	Wolf	Raven	Ash	ODIN	16.00	
RAIDO	Thunder	Journey	Hammer	Goat		Oak	THOR	17.00	
KAUNAZ	Discomfort	Illness	Torch		Night-owl	Pine	SKULD	18.00	Blue
GEBO	Gift		Glass	Oxen			GEFJUN	19.00	
WUNJO	Joy	Comfort	Drinkhorn					20.00	
HAGALAZ	Hail	Destruct					HELLA	21.00	Indigo
NAUTHIZ	Need	Constrain				Beech		22.00	

Figure 15. (a) A devotional framework constructed using the runes and some correspondences.

DEVOTIONAL FRAMEWORK 2

Rune Group	Moon Phase	Festival	Direction	Element	Day	Fest.Time
ISA JERA EIWAZ	New Moon	Winter Solstice	North	Earth	Wednesday	Midnight
PERTHO ALGIZ SOWULO		Feb Eve	North-east	Earth/Air	Friday	Small hours
TEIWAZ BERKANA EHWAZ	Waxing Moon	Spring Equinox	East	Air	Sunday	Dawn
MANNAZ LAGUZ INGUZ		May Eve	South-east	Air/Fire	Thursday	Morning
OTHILA DAGAZ FEHU	Full Moon	Summer Solstice	South	Fire	Saturday	Noon
URUZ THURISAZ ANSUZ		August Eve	South-west	Fire/Water		Afternoon
RAIDO KAUNAZ GEBO	Waning Moon	Autumn Equinox	West	Water	Tuesday	Sunset
WUNJO HAGALAZ NAUTHIZ		Nov Eve	North-west	Water/Earth	Monday	Evening

Figure 15. (b)

may observe, and, if you prefer, your own personal 'Sunday', on whatever day of the week it happens to fall. The daily ones will essentially be private, before a personal shrine, altar or icon (perhaps a sculpture, painting or drawing of your preferred deity), with a little incense (pine resin is an easily-obtainable and very appropriate incense, rather than frankincense or some other Mediterranean or exotic fume) and a lighted candle burning to their honour.

An Example

Assume someone has selected Skadi as a patron. Skadi was briefly and unsatisfactorily married to Njord, whom she selected, thinking he was Baldur, in a 'beautiful feet' competition. She is the hunting goddess, an equivalent of the Greek Artemis or the Roman Diana, at home in cold climes.

Taking September 1992 as an example, here is a way in which our Skadi-worshipper might elect to structure a scheme of personal devotion:

5th Saturday	First quarter
7th Monday	Skadi's Day
	Runes appropriate: *Wunjo, Hagalaz, Nauthiz*
	Direction: North-west
	Time of feast: Evening/21.00
	Elements appropriate: Water/Earth
	Robe/Cloth colour: Indigo
	Moon ideally: Waning to dark
12th Saturday	Full moon
14th Monday	Skadi's Day
	Ritual devised from the material given on Monday 7th above. This may be adapted depending upon the phase of the moon at the time of working.
19th Saturday	Last quarter
21st Monday	Skadi's Day Autumn equinox
	The Skadi's Day ritual should be adapted to suit the occasion by using the appropriate information from the autumn equinox entry on the framework:

Runes appropriate:	*Raido, Kaunaz, Gebo*
Direction:	West
Time of festival:	Sunset/18.00
Element appropriate:	Water
Deity:	Skuld
Moon phase:	Waning
Robe/Cloth colour:	Blue
26th Saturday	New Moon
28th Monday	Skadi's Day

The personal Skadi's Day devotions would be built up out of the elements taken from the framework entry against her name, as would any celebrated for the lunar phases or the major festivals. The actual content will naturally vary from person to person.

8 · USING THE RUNES TODAY

RUNES AND HEALING

Various schemes have been put forward to attribute some of the runes to parts of the body, and there is no doubt from the evidence given in the eddas and sagas that runes were employed in curative magic. Several charms have been preserved and handed down to us, and it is largely because of this that these attempts have been made.

The list which follows is an attempt to reconstruct this usage based on edda and saga information together with glosses from the runic poems. The list is accurate in theory but has yet to be fully medically proven.

FEHU	The chest, respiratory complaints.
URUZ	Bodily musculature, strength etc.
THURISAZ	The heart.
ANSUZ	The mouth, the teeth, speech disorders.
RAIDO	The legs and buttocks.
KAUNAZ	Ulcers, fevers, abscesses and so on.
GEBO	Poisoning.
WUNJO	Breathing disorders, relief of pain generally.
HAGALAZ	Wounds, cuts and blood disorders.
NAUTHIZ	The arms.

ISA	Frostbite, paralysis, loss of sensation.
JERA	Bowel conditions, digestive disorders.
EIHWAZ	Eye conditions.
PERTHO	The female breasts and genitalia, birth.
ALGIZ	The head and brain, insanity.
SOWULO	Burns and skin disorders.
TEIWAZ	The wrists, hands and fingers, arthritis.
BERKANA	Various problems connected with fertility.
EHWAZ	Back pains, problems and conditions.
MANNAZ	The feet and ankles, including sprains.
LAGUZ	Problems and diseases of the kidneys and urination.
INGUZ	Diseases and problems of the male genitalia.
OTHILA	Inherited diseases and defects.
DAGAZ	Fear, mental illness and distress.

RUNES AND MEDITATION

Using individual runes, bind-runes and runic words and inscriptions for meditation and pathworkings can prove an extremely rewarding occupation. If you have built up your own set of runic correspondences, based on the devotional frameworks given above or other, more personal, research, you will have a series of concepts symbolized by each individual rune, or sequence of runes, which when used for meditation will serve unreservedly to enhance your knowledge.

These can be used in several ways. One is simply to visualize the rune and its associated symbols during a meditation, thus enhancing your appreciation of the individual rune's worth and your understanding of it. Another is to create a pathworking around the symbol which will take you into a deeper understanding of its meaning. A good way to do this is to plan the pathworking beforehand and either have it written out for a colleague to read or put certain keywords on tape, timed to remind you during the progress of the experience. A third is to take the rune as a sigil and use its power to some measurable advantage. Another is to take either the rune or the sequence and determine how it relates to you personally. You may wish to consider numerological, symbolic and personal attributes. The only limit to your use of the runes is that which may be imposed by your imagination.

RUNES AND THE ARTS

The angular shapes of the runes appear around you in a great many guises. For instance, if you are looking at a holiday brochure you may find the name 'Greece' spelled in angular letters. On the bus or driving into work you might see modern buildings designed on runic principles or even old, half-timbered structures with runic beam-shapes set into them. And many poems with runic references are to be found in the old literature of the north. Closer to modern times W.H. Auden, undoubtedly one of our greatest poets, was fascinated by things Norse and by Iceland in particular, and produced an excellent translation of many edda poems.

The runes can be around us in many more ways than we normally would perceive. They are our natural legacy, and as such may sometimes require an effort to identify. Yet the effort they require us to make serves only to help us to derive more from them. Anything given too easily is devalued.

RUNE CHARMS IN DAILY LIFE

Winning the pools is naturally impossible if you don't fill in a coupon. Even if you do there's no guarantee that putting *Fehu* instead of a cross will work. But some simple combinations of rune and number sequences may have a dramatic result upon your life. The numbers three and eight are known winners, whatever the vagaries of fate, and with the right runes in the right numerical combination you could be able to alter your life for ever.

SIGILS

A potent method of using the runes is to make them into a sigil on a hard object which will serve both to remind you of your objective and to assist you in gaining it. This is why Scirnir cut runes on the wand in *For Scirnis*. He needed to control Gerd and sought out the best way of doing it. Making a runic sigil (combination of signs) is an excellent way of assisting your desires to become reality.

RUNES, SIGILS AND SHAMANISM

The combination of a system of magic like the runes with an apparently less-formalized practice such as shamanism might at first glance appear unlikely. Yet there is initial common ground in that neither possesses any demonstrable logical or scientific basis. Both appear to belong to a past time, not a vital present with its urgencies and requirements for streamlined and computerized efficiency.

And yet there are both similarities and possibilities for integration. The runes themselves, as we have seen, most probably derive from a North Italic alphabet and embody characteristics also found in both the Greek and Latin alphabets, linking them historically in a parallel development to Gnosticism. There is also strong reason to believe runic usage made input into both the medieval Goetia (the word literally means 'howling', and is used to described the sorcerous, Qabala-based magic of the grimoires or spell-books) and the separate but related traditions of witchcraft and sorcery, as well as contributing to the general development of which the eighteenth century sect of the Bavarian Illuminati was simply a single Teutonic manifestation.

The European witch cult was heavily influenced by the Northern Tradition and its material. In turn, both together and separately, the witch-cult and the separately-surviving Northern lore had an observable effect upon the Bavarian Illuminati. The same is true of the interchange of ideas and techniques related to sorcery, with northern methods infiltrating the practices in the same way that, reversing the process, the SATOR square is discovered in runic versions as early as the thirteenth century. And to ignore the shamanic roots of northern magical practice is implicitly to deny its influence, as if we were telling Siberian shamans they couldn't use the mushroom *Amanita Muscaria* for their rites.

Mastery of mind control

Runic was never a cursive script and remained epigraphic throughout its historical life, with the exception of some scholastic exercises which today have little value, as indeed was the case at the time (twelfth to thirteenth centuries) they were written. This implies that any teachings were passed on orally, and maintained and enhanced in the same fashion, requiring a substantial effort of mental recall.

Mastery of mind control involves a variety of methods which are used both by today's rune magician and by the shaman. Both motionlessness and breath control are basics of útiseta, the 'sitting out' which is used to set both the runic magician and the shaman apart from the world he or she normally inhabits. The resulting 'not-thinking' has the same intrinsic value for both rune magician and shaman, freeing body and mind and leading to the magical trance which is required to examine and explore the nine worlds of Norse creation.

Object concentration is a further basic for the dedicated rune magician and the shaman. But for the rune magician the object, which for the shaman may be a mark on the wall, something in the distance, a star in the night and so on, is better defined and always to hand. The object is a rune, with its attendant correspondences and implications.

The angular shapes of the runes, designed to be cut rather than written and, as such, alien to those of us accustomed to curves and right angles in our alphabet, add an otherness to their use which successfully sets them apart from normal writing in the same way that shamanic symbols and, in our own century, Austin Osman Spare's 'Alphabet of Desire', are set apart. The advantage of the runes is that they prevent the need for an antidote to the imbalance which could result from entering a magical trance, any possible side-effect being immediately countered by referring the individual symbol to its position in the futhark.

But the runes, however useful they may be as aids in processes of training and meditation, are essentially a magical system, comprising twenty-four tools which can be used singly or in combination, either as words, sequences or sigils, to create specified and desired effects. Even the construction of sigils as originally expounded by Austin Osman Spare acquires an unwonted facility which might otherwise prove illusive if the runes, with their angular shapes facilitating sigilization, are employed. Shamanism however, depending as it does upon ecstatic techniques, has less use for sigils or other drawn, carved or painted characters.

RUNIC CODES

The division of the futhark into *aettir* gave rise to several varieties of cryptic, or coded, forms of rune with which anyone writing in runes could guard his or her message from anyone who might know the original symbols but didn't possess the key to the code. The usual method was to take either a plain vertical stave or a simple drawing of an object and place strokes to either side of it to represent the *aett* and the position of the letter within the *ætt*. For example:

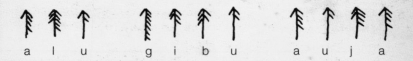

Another idea was to use a drawing of a bearded face and alter the lines representing the hairs on the beard to identify the position and *ætt* of each rune represented:

There was also the practice of creating bind-runes, which could be undertaken for at least three distinct purposes:

1. Shorthand, combining two adjacent runes on the same stave to save either time or space.
2. Cryptography, to mystify one untutored in the process and prevent the inscription being properly understood.
3. Magic, which could combine the the first two purposes to ensure that a spell remained secret and thus more potent.

Another common practice was to use single runes for their name-words, or as abbreviations for other words, either in secular or magical inscriptions. We noticed an example of this earlier with the bracteate from Poznan in Poland, where the inscription 'wise one rune [s]' is made up like this:

s   a   b   a   r

– with *saba* meaning 'wise one' and 'r' meaning 'rune[s]'.

Another example, illustrating both initials standing for words and the use of a bind-rune, is the combination of the two words *Gibu* and *Auja* used to show types of cryptic rune above. Together the two mean '[I] give [good] luck', and the initials combined into one symbol have been found on several objects in this form as well as written out in full.

THE RUNES AND THE QABALA

Anyone interested in the runes very probably has at least a passing acquaintance with magical and self-development matters. If this is so then the term 'Qabala', however spelled, won't be too foreign. The Qabala is a system of mystical thought which maps out the universe using a diagram called the Tree of Life and the letters of the Hebrew alphabet. The letters are used as keys upon which a collection of correspondences are built up, such as deities, perfumes, objects, plants, animals and so on. This is also possible for the runes, which share with the Hebrew alphabet a characteristic not found anywhere else in the northern hemisphere.

Like the Hebrew alphabet, the runic letters have name-words with meanings in their own right. Thus the Hebrew G is *Gimel*, a camel, and the runic G is *Gebo*, a gift, with name and meaning pairings extending through both alphabets. There is also another similarity, albeit more tenuous, in that the Qabala uses the Tree of Life and Norse mythology centres around the world ash-tree, Yggdrasil.

Here the similarities end, though, as much because of the climatic differences in which the two cultures originated as for any other reason. The Hebrews dwelled in desert lands, whereas the northern peoples lived in a much colder but equally hostile environment.

WICCA

Another system which must be briefly examined, if we are to do justice to the role of the number eight in runecraft, is the eightfold wheel of Wicca. The Alexandrian and Gardnerian movements represent the bulk of more obvious modern witch-craft activity, and are twentieth century offshoots of a tradition going back much further and represented by the hereditary and traditional schools, both of which are realities in England today. Unlike the latter two they are visible and (heresy coming up) virtually interchangeable.

This does not take us too far from the point, as both the Alexandrians and the Gardnerians have been keen in recent years to establish their respectability and credentials, even permitting a degree of cooperation and interpenetration in order to do so. A variety of eight-spoked wheel diagrams are to be found in the plethora of works about either or both. They typically contain:

FESTIVALS	METHODOLOGY	WEAPONRY
Candlemas	Drugs and wine	Bread
Vernal equinox	Dance	Wand/Staff
Beltane	Great Rite	Incense
Summer solstice	Spells and rites	Athame/Knife
Lammas	Scourge	Wine
Autumnal equinox	Cords	Chalice/Cup
Samhain	Meditation	Oil
Winter solstice	Trance	Pentacle/Plate

Naturally this is a synthesis and there are omissions. But it serves to provide a general idea for anyone new to the idea of the eight-fold division of the year.

9 · THE FUTURE OF THE RUNES

The present revival of the Northern Tradition, of which the runes will always be the undoubted cornerstone, is of necessity a continuing process. The myths regarding the so-called Armanen runes which were perpetuated by Guido von List and others, even in our own time, have been shattered by the evidence of scholarship and archaeology and, save in the works of a few misguided persons, persist only as curiosities, like the medieval runic manuscripts.

COMMON SENSE

The important role which remains for the old northern culture to play is one of guidance. In poems such as *Hávamál* there is a wealth of lore to be explored and discovered, much of it still highly relevant to modern life. For instance, it contains a series of verses which offer good advice to many, including these:

> Not too much care but care enough:
> Drink ale not in excess;
> Be wary of another's wife,
> And trust not tricks of thieves.

> With a good man talk is good,
> Find in him firm a friend:
> But waste no words on witless ones,
> With stupidity sit not down.

There are many more, still valid today if we can look past their archaic language. These two alone caution us against too much booze, becoming involved with the wives of others, falling for deceptions and choosing the wrong people for our friends. Many of the other poems and tales from the eddas and sagas also hold important information we can benefit from, even on the most basic level of our daily mundane lives.

RELIGION

The old religion of the north is still firmly with us today. In a revived form it has been an official alternative state religion in Iceland for nearly two decades now and has manifested in other countries as diverse as Scandinavia and the United States. Asatrú ('the truth or troth of the Aesir') is one of the commonest alternative pagan religions of Northern Europe, including the British Isles.

Norse paganism is demonstrably older than Wicca. The latter retained many of its teachings but, in being forced underground without its original writings being preserved, is available to the majority today in the form in which Gerald Gardner recreated it, with the paid assistance of Aleister Crowley, during the Second World War. The few that have preserved its teachings through transmission via the family (hereditary witches) are not talking. Neither are the traditional covens from which Gardner drew his material.

As an existing faith in England, Norse paganism is represented by several charitable organizations. If you are interested in exploring this further contact the Odinic Rite at:

B M EDDA
London WC1N 3XX

One of the best teaching grounds for Odinism, Asatrú, or whatever the old religion of the north is named in this country, is the Asatrú Folk Runic Workshop, which is run by Freya Aswynn. This offers a correspondence course in runes and the Northern Mysteries which goes way beyond the material covered in this book. Those interested should send a stamped-addressed envelope to:

B M ASWYNN
London WC1N 3XX

Alternatively you might choose to examine the faith by reading the eddas and sagas and coming to your own conclusions with like-minded friends (shades of the *Hávamál* verse given above). For many people this is bound to be the best alternative, providing as it does access to original material, albeit with Christian bias in places, which will permit the reconstruction of those aspects of the faith which they require. While I am not presently teaching runecraft or doing castings for other people I will try to answer any questions you may have if you write to me via the publishers of this book.

Personally, since that violently windy night on which I first discovered the power of Odin in 1963, it is impossible for me to profess any other faith. The old gods are alive and well and living in every tree and stone and brook and field around me. My home town was an administrative centre for the Danelaw, and I've taken my tradition from the ground on which I stand.

THE RAGNARÖK

One last observation, the famous Ragnarök, or Doom of the Norse Gods, appears in the eddas and sagas only as a prophecy. It was spoken by a *völva* to Odin in the poem *Völuspá*.

Given the power of the gods, and not forgetting that Odin gave one of his eyes in exchange for greater than mortal wisdom, there is no reason why he should not have found a way to circumvent his own destruction. When Iceland converted to Christianity on 4 June 1000 it was essentially as an act of pragmatism, to save Icelandic hostages held by the Christian Norwegian King Olaf Tryggveson, who was threatening to kill them if the conversion did not take place. Olaf is now only a name from history and was killed in a sea-battle later the same year, whilst Odin and the others are already back home in an official capacity. With this in mind we should not deny the potency and relevance of the Old Faith of the North, both for past times and our own.

GLOSSARY

Æsir: A plural word meaning the Old Norse Gods of the family of which Odin was the patriarch. The singular is Ase.

Ætt/Ættir: Ætt is the singular, ættir the plural. An ætt was one of three groups of letters which together made up the runic alphabet. The Common Germanic Futhark was made up of three groups, or ættir, of eight runes to a group.

Allfather: One of the titles of Odin.

Asatrú: An Icelandic word meaning 'belief in the Æsir'.

Asgard: The home of the Æsir. It contained many palaces occupied by the Gods and Goddesses as well as Valhalla, the 'Hall of the Slain' where dead warriors were taken.

Asvid: A ruler of the giants.

Aurochs: The extinct wild ox of Europe, last seen alive in 1627. Caesar described them as very large and fierce.

Austri: The name of one of the four dwarves who held up the sky in Norse myth. It means 'from the east'. The other three were Nordri, Sudri and Vestri.

Bestla: Odin's mother. The name has never been satisfactorily translated.

Bolthorn: Literally 'Evil Thorn', a giant and Odin's grandfather.

Bracteate: A small medallion of precious metal usually made to resemble an ancient coin.

Chape: A trimming or decoration which also normally performs some function. A scabbard-chape, for instance, will both decorate the scabbard and prevent the weapon it contains cutting through the leather.

Dain: A ruler of the elves.

Delling: Literally 'day-spring', the dawn.

Deosil: Clockwise movement, with the sun as opposed to against it.

Dvalin: A ruler of the dwarves.

Edda(s): There are two collections of Old Norse material known as eddas. The 'Prose Edda' is the work of Snorri Sturluson, who wrote it some time before 1235. Twice Lawspeaker of Iceland, he was murdered for political reasons in 1241. The 'Verse' or 'Elder Edda' is a collection of heroic and mythological poems, some of which can be dated back to around AD 900. Both are fascinating reading.

Equinox: The time of the year when day and night are of equal length.

Galdr: One of the two principal forms of Norse magic. Galdr was the magic of verse and incantations, linking the magic of poetry to runecraft, etc. It was Æsir magic as opposed to Vanir magic.

Hällristningar: Symbols from Bronze Age rock carvings found throughout Scandinavia and usually regarded as the forerunners of the runic symbols.

Hávamál: One of the poems of the *Elder Edda*, allegedly containing the words of Odin himself. Part of it, known as the *Runatál*, contains a great deal of the surviving runelore.

Heimskringla: A book by Snorri Sturluson giving the history of the kings of Norway from the earliest (mythological) times to 1177.

Hvitakrist: Literally 'White Christ', the term used by Christian missionaries to describe the new God who was inexorably moving into Scandinavia from the south.

Loddfafnir: A skald, or poet, to whom Odin is singing in the Runatál.

Midgard: The material universe, which man inhabits.

Monkalpha: The Latin alphabet brought to the north by Christian missionary monks.

Nid: An insult which is also a curse. 'Niding' is the worst thing any northerner could be called. Egil Skallagrimsson set up a 'nid-pole' to magically banish Erik Bloodaxe from Norway. It worked.

Nine Worlds: The world-ash tree Yggdrasil contains the whole of creation, embraced by nine worlds. These are: Asgard, Hel (the norse underworld, and not to be confused with the Christian Hell), Jötunheim (Giant-home), Ljósálfheim (Light-Elf home), Midgard, Múspellheim (realm of fire), Niflheim (realm of ice), Svartálfheim (Dark-Elf home) and Vanaheim (home of the Vanir).

Norn: Usually taken as the singular of the Nornir, the three 'Fates' of Norse myth known as Urd, Verdandi and Skuld and representing past, present and future. There were other lesser Nornir as well.

Odrærir: The Mead of Poetry which Odin stole from Suttung's daughter. The myth is recounted in the *Hávamál*.

Primsigning: An agreement to think about becoming a baptized Christian which Norsemen undertook in order to trade with Christian communities.

Ragnarök: The 'Outcome of Destiny', usually taken as the passing of the old Norse pantheon in violent conflict with its enemies. While it has inspired much speculation as to when or if it happened it exists in Norse literature only as a prophecy.

Runatál: See *Hávamál*.

Saga(s): The sagas are family histories or novels, mostly written by medieval Icelanders, containing a great deal of information about the beliefs, lifestyle and customs of the pagan period.

Seidr: The magic of the Vanir taught to Odin by Freya. Because of its reliance on debilitating trance-states it was regarded as 'unmanly' for warriors to practise it.

Sigrdrifomál: A poem from the *Elder Edda* in which a Valkyrie reveals charms to the hero who rescues her.

Skald: An Old Norse word for a poet.

Solstice: The longest or shortest day of the year.

Thjodrerir: A dwarf mentioned in passing in one of the Runatál charms.

Thund: Another name for Odin.

Vanir: The Old Norse Gods and Goddesses of the family which centred around Njord, Frey and Freya. They tend on the whole to be more gentle and concerned with matters of fertility than the Æsir.

Völuspa: A poem from the *Elder Edda* in which a *Völva*, commanded by Odin, foressees the *Ragnarök*.

Völva: A seer, usually female and an exponent of *Seidr*.

Widdershins: The opposite of *Deosil*, moving counter-clockwise or against the sun.

Wyrd: The more common Anglo-Saxon form of the Old Norse concept of *Örlög*, meaning destiny, doom or fate.

Yggdrasil: The world-ash tree of Norse myth, containing the *Nine Worlds* and all that inhabits them.

BIBLIOGRAPHY

Those works marked * are particularly worth the newcomer's attention, either because they provide more information about the religion of the north or for additional information on runecraft and northern magic.

Antonsen, Elmer H. *A Concise Grammar of the Older Runic Inscriptions*, Tübingen, 1975.

* Aswynn, Freya *Leaves of Yggdrasil*, St Paul, 1990.

Aswynn, Freya and King, Bernard *Runes and the Northern Mysteries Correspondence Course*, London, 1991–1993.

* Branston, Brian *Gods of the North*, London, 1955.

* Branston, Brian *The Lost Gods of England*, London, 1957.

* Bray, Olive *The Elder or Poetic Edda*, London, 1908.

Cockayne, Reverend Oswald *Leechdoms, Wortcunning and Starcraft of Early England*, London, 1864.

* Davidson, H.R. Ellis *Gods and Myths of Northern Europe*, Harmondsworth, 1964.

Davidson, H.R. Ellis *Myths and Symbols in Pagan Europe*, Manchester, 1988.

Dickins, Bruce *Runic and Heroic Poems of the Old Teutonic Peoples*, Cambridge, 1915.

Dumézil, Georges *Gods of the Ancient Northmen*, California, 1977.

* Elliott, Ralph W.V. *Runes, An Introduction*, Manchester, 1959

Evans, D.H. (ed) *Hávamál*, London, 1986.

Faulkes, Anthony (ed). *Edda*, London, 1988.

Gelling, Peter and Davidson, Hilda Ellis *The Chariot of the Sun*, London, 1969.

* Guerber, H.A. *Myths of the Norsemen*, London, 1919.

Gundarsson, Kveldulf *Teutonic Magic*, St Paul, 1990.

Haugen, Einer, *The Scandinarian Languages*, London, 1976.

Hodgetts, J. Frederick *Older England* (Second Series), London, 1884.

Jansson, Sven B.F. *Runes in Sweden*, Sweden, 1987.

Jóhannesson, Jón (trans. Haraldur Bessasson) *A History of the Old Icelandic Commonwealth*, Manitoba, 1974.

Johnson, Walter *Byways in British Archaeology*, Cambridge, 1912.

King, Bernard *Ultima Thule: The Vanished Northern Homeland*, London, 1992.

Larson, G.J. *Myth in Indo-European Antiquity*, California, 1974.

Leland, Charles G. *Gypsy Sorcery and Fortune Telling*, London, 1891.

* Mackenzie, Donald A. *Teutonic Myth and Legend*, London n.d.

Mallet, M. (trans. Percy) *Northern Antiquities*, London, 1902.

Moltke, Erik *Runes and Their Origins*, Copenhagen, 1985.

Musset, Lucien *Introduction á la Runologie*, Paris, 1965.

* Page, R. I. *An Introduction to English Runes*, London, 1973.

* Pennick, Nigel *Practical Magic in the Northern Tradition*, Wellingborough, 1989.

Randsborg, Klavs *The Viking Age in Denmark*, London, 1980.

Rodrigues, Louis J. *Anglo-Saxon Verse Runes*, Felinfach, 1992.

Reuter, Otto Siegfried 'Sky Lore of the North' in *Stonehenge Viewpoint*, Santa Barbara, 1982.

Scherman, Katharine *Iceland, Daughter of Fire*, London, 1976.

Spare, Austin Osman, *The Book of Pleasure*, Northampton, 1987.

Storms, Gustav, *Anglo-Saxan Magic*, The Hague, 1948.

Ström, Folke *Nid, Ergi and Old Norse Moral Attitudes* London, 1974.

Sturluson, Snorri *Ynglinga Saga in Heimskringla*, London, 1930.

* Tacitus, P. Cornelius *The Agricola* and *The Germania*, Harmondsworth, 1948.

Talley, Jeannine E. *Runes, Mandrakes and Gallows* in G.J. Larson.

* Terry, Patricia *Poems of the Vikings*, Indianapolis, 1969.

* Thorsson, Edred *Runelore*, York Beach, 1987.

* Young, Jean I. *The Prose Edda of Snorri Sturluson*, Cambridge, 1954.

INDEX